The Neolithic Flint Mines of England

ENGLISH HERITAGE

The Neolithic Flint Mines of England

Martyn Barber, David Field and Peter Topping

ROYAL COMMISSION ON THE HISTORICAL MONUMENTS OF ENGLAND

Published by English Heritage at the National Monuments Record Centre, Great Western Village, Kemble Drive, Swindon SN2 2GZ

© English Heritage 1999
Images (except as otherwise shown) © Crown copyright 1999

Applications for the reproduction of images should be made to the National Monuments Record

The Royal Commission on the Historical Monuments of England and English Heritage merged on 1 April 1999

First published 1999

ISBN 1 873592 41 8

British Library Cataloguing in Publication Data
A CIP catalogue record for this book is available from the British Library

Designed by Chuck Goodwin, 27 Artesian Road, London W2 5DA

Printed in Belgium by Snoeck-Ducaju & Zoon

Contents

Acknowledgements

Many members of staff have assisted with this study, either with the fieldwork and the reports that were generated, or with the preparation of this book. Graham Brown, Moraig Brown, Jo Donachie, Jane Kenney, David McOmish, Al Oswald, Paul Pattison, Trevor Pearson and Paul Struth all assisted with field survey, while Deborah Cunliffe, Al Oswald and Trevor Pearson prepared the illustrations. The latter also prepared computer-aided illustrations. Carolyn Dyer plotted the sites at Blackpatch and Stoke Down from air photographs. Photography was by Steven Cole and Alun Bull. David Ride assisted with field survey at Martin's Clump and Easton Down. The staff at English Heritage's visitor centre at Grime's Graves were particularly helpful during the course of survey work.

We would like to thank all the landowners and tenants, too numerous to mention individually, who allowed access to sites. The National Trust and the Forestry Commission were also supportive and allowed access to sites in their charge.

Museum and library staff provided valuable help, particularly Sally White of Worthing Museum & Art Gallery; the Sussex Archaeological Society at Barbican House, Lewes; Pamela Wace at the Baden Powell Quaternary Research Centre, Oxford; Janet Bell at Salisbury Museum; Ros Cleal and Clare Coneybeare at the Alexander Keiller Museum, Avebury; and the staff at Norwich, Thetford, Bury St Edmunds and Brighton Museums.

In addition we would like to thank Frances Healy, Robin Holgate, Ian Kinnes, Roger Mercer, Alan Saville and Gillian Varndell for much correspondence and comment upon the results of the project.

The British Museum kindly agreed to run a small programme of radiocarbon dates and we would like to thank Janet Ambers for assisting with this; Alex Bayliss of the Ancient Monuments Laboratory provided calibrations of other radiocarbon dates; Dale Serjeantson of the University of Southampton recorded the animal bone before destruction.

Versions of the text have been read and commented upon by Professor Richard Bradley, Humphrey Welfare, Paul Everson and Robin Taylor. Robin Taylor, Diane Williams and Elizabeth Nichols provided editorial assistance and the index was prepared by Susanne Atkin. The French and German summaries were prepared by SR Translations, with assistance from Gillian Varndell and Susan McNeil.

English Heritage is grateful to the following for allowing permission to reproduce photographs and illustrations: The British Museum: Figs 2.9, 5.9; Mrs B Heryet and Worthing Museum & Art Gallery: Fig 2.8; Sussex Archaeological Society: Figs 2.5, 5.8; Norfolk Record Office: Fig 2.1; and Mrs M Suckling: Fig 2.7. The contour information on the maps and plans is derived from 1:10 000 Ordnance Survey maps.

Summary

Neolithic flint mines represent some of the longest-surviving earthworks to be seen in the modern English landscape. However, despite a lengthy history of archaeological investigation, they have rarely been considered nationally as a class of monument. Although some sites such as Grime's Graves are well known through recent excavation campaigns, others are known only through obscure articles and unpublished archival material. Many of those that survive as earthworks or cropmarks have never previously been surveyed or accurately planned.

This project comprised a programme of surveys incorporating analytical field investigation, aerial photography and archival research. The aim was to provide a full and detailed account of what is known and what survives, in order to meet the growing needs of professional archaeologists, site managers, conservation bodies, and the informed general reader. Considering the mines from a landscape perspective, integrating the results of detailed fieldwork with the documentary and archival sources, enables a more complete picture of these sites to be constructed, and offers an improved understanding of their roles within prehistory as well as their importance today. The project is particularly timely as few mines survive as earthworks, and some continue to suffer from unsympathetic land use. In addition to the Neolithic sites, one of the few partly surviving post-medieval gunflint sites, at Lingheath Farm, Brandon in Suffolk, was also selected for survey. This site provided a well-documented example of a method of flint extraction, which could offer a useful comparison with the Neolithic mines.

A brief history of archaeological investigation of flint mines places past excavations and interpretations into a broader context of changing academic and interpretative frameworks. Only ten sites have in fact produced evidence for Neolithic extraction, while another two seem highly probable, but lack definite evidence. Among the forty-four rejected are some of the most frequently mentioned in the archaeological literature, such as Great Massingham in Norfolk, and Windover Hill in East Sussex.

It seems clear that the placing of mines in the landscape was not determined solely by the location of the best quality or most easily accessible flint. Mining is so far only attested on the South Downs of southern England, the eastern fringe of Salisbury Plain and in East Anglia, with two basic landscape positions evident – some occupy prominent skyline locations, others are relatively hidden by the local topography. The lack of evidence for contemporary structures at mines underlines the difficulties involved in understanding both the practicalities of flint extraction and any 'domestic' activity associated with the mining. Although some excavations have uncovered evidence for contemporary activity, which does not necessarily form part of the extractive process, the role and nature of this activity remains unclear. The presence of placed deposits at Grime's Graves in particular highlights the occurrence of 'ritual' practices within the 'industrial' processes. The scale of extraction was not intensive in a modern, commercial sense, although the complexity and scale of surviving earthworks, and estimates of the amount of flint extracted, may appear to suggest otherwise. The detailed radiocarbon chronology for Grime's Graves, for example, need require no more than one shaft per year to have been dug. During and after the use of these sites for mining, they represented important places in the cultural landscape, attracting special deposits, funerary activity and monument construction as well as acting as sources for flint from spoil heaps, or places for the deposition of midden material.

The project identified several areas where further work is required. There is a clear need for a more refined chronology for flint mining within the Neolithic. Although Grime's Graves has numerous dates from secure contexts, the same cannot be said of the other mines. During the project, the small number of dates available for the South Downs sites was complemented by a few more, kindly provided by the British Museum, derived from artefacts from old excavations. These dates confirm that mining was underway at these sites during the early 4th millennium BC, in contrast to activity, predominantly of the 3rd millennium BC, at Grime's Graves.

Carefully-targeted excavation, along with fieldwalking and geophysical survey could assist in a number of important areas, including determining the extent of mine complexes, obtaining datable material, understanding the environmental context of the mines, and discovering more about extraction techniques. There is a particular need for the large quantities of unpublished information to be more widely disseminated. The full publication of earlier excavations and other fieldwork is essential, as is additional research to re-evaluate the results of earlier published excavations. It is also essential to stress the rarity and fragility of these sites, and to highlight the need for sympathetic land use to aid their conservation and preservation.

Résumé

Les mines de silex du néolithique font partie des plus anciens ouvrages de terre que conserve le paysage anglais moderne. Cependant, en dépit d'une longue histoire de fouilles archéologiques, elles ont rarement été considérées sur le plan national comme constituant une catégorie de monuments à proprement parler. Bien que certains sites, comme Grime's Graves, aient gagné en notoriété par des campagnes de fouilles récentes, d'autres ne sont connus que par le biais d'articles obscurs ou mentionnés dans des archives non publiées. Beaucoup de ceux qui survivent sous la forme d'ouvrages de terre ou de marques au sol n'ont jamais fait l'objet d'étude ni de relevé précis.

Ce projet s'est accompagné d'un programme d'études incluant des fouilles analytiques sur le terrain, des photographies aériennes et des recherches à partir d'archives. L'objectif était de fournir un compte-rendu complet et détaillé de ce qui est connu et de ce qui subsiste pour répondre aux besoins croissants des archéologues professionnels, des directeurs de sites, des organismes de protection et plus généralement du lecteur informé. Le fait d'envisager les mines à partir du paysage, et d'intégrer les résultats d'un travail sur le terrain approfondi aux sources documentaires et aux archives disponibles, permet d'élaborer une perspective plus complète sur ces sites et de mieux comprendre tant leurs rôles à l'époque préhistorique que leur importance aujourd'hui. Le projet est arrivé à point nommé car il reste peu de mines sous la forme d'ouvrages de terre et certaines continuent de pâtir d'un usage du sol qui leur est peu favorable. En plus des sites néolithiques, l'un des rares sites de silex à fusil de l'époque post médiévale qui subsiste, celui de Lingheath Farm, Brandon dans le comté du Suffolk, a lui aussi été sélectionné pour faire partie de l'étude. Ce site a fourni un exemple bien documenté d'une méthode d'extraction du silex, qui offre une comparaison appréciable par rapport aux mines néolithiques.

Un bref historique des fouilles archéologiques des mines de silex situe les fouilles et les interprétations passées dans un contexte plus large où les structures académiques et d'interprétation sont en mutation. Dix sites seulement ont fourni des preuves d'une extraction néolithique, bien que deux autres semblent fortement probables mais manquent de preuves irréfutables. Parmi les quarante quatre sites rejetés, quelques-uns font partie des sites les plus fréquemment mentionnés dans les publications archéologiques, comme Great Massingham dans le Norfolk et Windover Hill dans l'East Sussex.

Il semble clair que l'emplacement des mines dans le paysage n'était pas uniquement déterminé par le fait qu'il s'y trouvait du silex de la meilleure qualité ou d'un accès facile. L'attestation de la présence d'exploitation minière se limite jusqu'à présent aux collines du South Downs dans le sud de l'Angleterre, à la bordure orientale de la plaine de Salisbury, et dans la région d'East Anglia, se manifestant sous forme de deux situations géographiques principales : certains sites occupent des lieux proéminents se dégageant sur la ligne d'horizon, alors que d'autres sont relativement dissimulés par la topographie locale. L'absence de traces de structures contemporaines dans les mines souligne les difficultés rencontrées pour comprendre tant les aspects pratiques de l'extraction du silex que toute activité "domestique" associée à l'extraction minière. Bien que certaines fouilles aient révélé des traces d'activités contemporaines qui ne faisaient pas nécessairement partie du processus d'extraction, le rôle et la nature de ces activités restent flous. La présence de dépôts sur place, à Grime's Graves en particulier, met en lumière des pratiques "rituelles" qui avaient lieu au sein des processus "industriels". L'échelle d'extraction n'était pas ce qu'on appelle intensive dans un sens moderne et commercial, bien que la complexité et l'ampleur des ouvrages de terre qui subsistent, et l'évaluation des quantités de silex extraites, semblent montrer le contraire. La chronologie détaillée au carbone 14 pour Grime's Graves indique par exemple qu'il suffisait qu'un seul puits soit creusé par an. Pendant et après leur utilisation à des fins minières, ces sites représentaient de hauts lieux dans le paysage culturel, attirant des dépôts spéciaux, des activités funéraires et l'édification de monuments, en plus de servir de sources de silex à partir des amas de déchets ou comme lieu pour y déposer des ordures.

Le projet a relevé plusieurs domaines où de plus amples travaux sont nécessaires. Il ne fait pas de doute qu'il faut élaborer une chronologie plus précise de l'exploitation minière du silex au sein de la période néolithique. Bien que Grime's Graves comporte plusieurs datations à partir de contextes sûrs, il n'en va pas de même pour les autres mines. Au cours du projet, les rares dates disponibles pour les sites des South Downs ont été complétées par quelques dates supplémentaires gracieusement fournies par le British Museum, obtenues à partir d'artefacts provenant de fouilles précédentes. Ces dates confirment que l'exploitation de ces lieux a commencé au début du 4e millénaire av. J.-C., par contraste avec des activités principalement du 3e millénaire av. J.-C. à Grime's Graves.

Des fouilles minutieusement ciblées, ainsi que des arpentages sur place et des études géophysiques permettraient d'éclairer plusieurs points et, entre autres, de déterminer l'étendue des complexes miniers, d'obtenir des matériaux datables, de comprendre le contexte environnemental des mines et d'en savoir plus sur les techniques d'extraction employées. Il est tout particulièrement nécessaire de diffuser plus largement les grandes quantités d'informations non publiées. La publication complète des fouilles précédentes et d'autres travaux sur le terrain est primordiale ; il est par ailleurs nécessaire de procéder à de plus amples recherches pour réévaluer les résultats des fouilles précédentes qui ont fait l'objet de publications. Il est aussi capital d'insister sur la rareté et la fragilité de ces sites et de souligner la nécessité d'une utilisation des sols qui les respecte pour favoriser leur conservation et leur protection.

Übersicht

Feuersteingruben aus der Jungsteinzeit gehören zu den ältesten, noch erhalten gebliebenen Erdwallanhäufungen in der modernen englischen Kulturlandschaft. Man hat sie jedoch, trotz langer archäologischer Erforschung, selten als Altertumsdenkmäler eingestuft. Mehrere solcher Stätten, wie z. B. *Grime's Graves*, sind der Öffentlichkeit durch unlängst ausgeführte Ausgrabungen bekannt geworden. Daten über andere existieren lediglich in weniger bekannten Abhandlungen und als Archivmaterial. Viele Stätten, deren Form immer noch in Getreidefeldern oder als Erdwall erkennbar ist, sind bis heute noch nie erforscht oder genau vermessen worden.

Dieses Projekt hat Felderforschung, Luftaufnahmen und Archivrecherchen in einem Programm verbunden, und zwar mit dem Ziel, einen ausführlichen Bericht über Bekanntes und noch Erhaltenes zusammenzustellen, um den wachsenen Anforderungen von Archäologen, Verwaltungsbehörden, Altertums- und Naturschutzorganisationen sowie interessierten Lesern und Leserinnen gerecht zu werden. Die Gruben in ihrem landschaftlichen Rahmen und der Vergleich von Ergebnissen ausführlicher Felderforschung mit urkundlichen Quellen haben ein vollständigeres Bild dieser Stätten gegeben und somit ein besseres Verständnis ihrer vorgeschichtlichen Rolle und ihrer Bedeutung in der heutigen Zeit. Das Projekt ist zudem besonders aktuell, weil heute nur noch wenige Gruben als Erdwallanhäufungen erhalten sind und andere unter gleichgültiger Landnutzung gelitten haben. Außer den jungsteinzeitlichen Stätten wurde in diesem Forschungsprogramm auch eine noch teilweise erhaltene Grube, auf *Lingheath Farm* in Brandon, in der Grafschaft Sussex, vermessen, weil sie in der Neuzeit zur Förderung von Feuerstein für Steinschloßgewehre genutzt wurde. Die Forschungsergebnisse dieser Stätte bieten ein gut dokumentiertes Muster einer Feuersteinfördermethode, das als Vergleich für jungsteinzeitliche Gruben genutzt werden könnte.

Die kurze, zusammenfassende Geschichte der archäologischen Erforschung von Feuersteingruben bringt ältere Ausgrabungen und Interpretationen in einen Zusammenhang mit der sich ändernden akademischen Auslegung. Nur an zehn Grabungsstätten sind tatsächlich Beweise für jungsteinzeitliche Förderung gefunden worden, und an zwei Stätten kann eine solche Förderung trotz mangelnder Beweise mit aller Wahrscheinlichkeit vermutet werden. Unter den 44 für untauglich gefundenen Stätten sind mehrere, die in der Fachliteratur immer wieder beschrieben worden sind, z. B. *Great Massingham* in der Grafschaft Norfolk und *Windover Hill* in East Sussex.

Es scheint klar zu sein, daß ein Grubengelände nicht nur durch das Vorkommen eines qualitätvollen Feuersteins oder durch leichte Förderung bestimmt wurde. Feuersteinförderung kann gegenwärtig nur auf den *South Downs* in Südengland, dem östlichen Randgebiet der *Salisbury Plain* und in der Grafschaft East Anglia nachgewiesen werden. Zwei grundlegende landschaftliche Merkmale sind augenscheinlich: deutliche

Sichtbarkeit am Horizont oder eine relativ versteckte Lage in der lokalen Topographie. Mangelnde Funde zeitgenössischer Anlagen in den Gruben unterstreichen das problematische Verständnis der praktischen Feuersteinförderung und der „häuslichen", mit der Förderung zusammenhängenden Tätigkeiten. An mehreren Ausgrabungsstätten sind zwar Spuren für eine zeitgenössische Betätigung gefunden worden, die nicht unbedingt ein Teil des Förderprozesses gewesen war, aber die Rolle dieser Betätigung bleibt im wesentlichen unklar. Zurückgelassene Gegenstände in *Grime's Grave* deuten auf das Vorkommen „ritueller" Bräuche innerhalb des „industriellen" Prozesses. Die Ausbeutung war nicht intensiv im modernen, kommerziellen Sinn, obwohl die Komplexität und der Umfang der noch erhaltenen Erdwälle und Schätzungen der Fördermenge das Gegenteil andeuten. An der ausführlichen Radiokarbon-Chronologie der Stätte *Grime's Graves* ist z. B. festgestellt worden, daß nicht mehr als ein Schacht pro Jahr ausgehoben werden mußte. Während und nach der Nutzung dieser Stätten als Gruben, spielten sie eine bedeutende Rolle in der Kulturlandschaft und dienten als Lagerstätten für zurückgelassene Gegenstände, zur Beisetzung, zum Denkmalbau und ferner zum Sammeln von Feuersteinbrocken aus Kippen oder als Stätten für Kehrichthaufen.

Das Projekt hat verschiedene Bereiche identifiziert, wo weiter geforscht werden müßte. Eine viel ausführlichere Chronologie der Feuersteinförderung in der Jungsteinzeit sollte zusammengestellt werden. Für die Stätte *Grime's Grave* stehen zahlreiche Daten aus sicheren Quellen zur Verfügung; von den anderen Gruben kann das jedoch nicht behauptet werden. Während des Projekts konnten die wenigen bekannten Daten für die South-Down-Stätten durch einige mehr bereichert werden, die das Britische Museum zur Verfügung stellte und die Gebrauchsgegenstände datieren, die aus alten Ausgrabungen stammen. Diese Daten bestätigen, daß Feuerstein an diesen Stätten schon im 4. Jahrtausend v. Chr. gefördert wurde, im Gegensatz zu Vorgängen in *Grime's Grave*, die größtenteils auf das 3. Jahrtausend v. Chr. festgelegt werden können.

Gezielte Grabungen, Feldbegehung und geophysikalische Vermessungen könnten in vielen bedeutenden Bereichen nützlich sein, u. a. bei der Festlegung des Umfangs der Grubenkomplexe, bei der Verschaffung von datierbarem Material, zum besseren Verständnis der Grubenumgebung und um mehr über Fördertechniken zu erfahren. Die zahlreichen unveröffentlichten Informationen müßten an ein breiteres Publikum gelangen. Die vollständige Publikation älterer Ausgrabungen und weitere Felderforschung ist von größter Notwendigkeit, genau wie zusätzliche Recherchen, um die Ergebnisse älterer veröffentlichter Ausgrabungen neu zu bewerten. Es ist ferner geboten, die Seltenheit und Fragilität dieser Stätten zu betonen und eine verständnisvolle Landnutzung zu ihrer Erhaltung zu fordern.

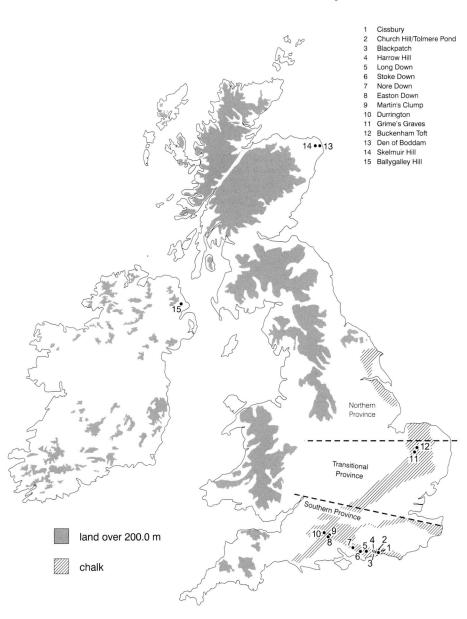

1   Cissbury
2   Church Hill/Tolmere Pond
3   Blackpatch
4   Harrow Hill
5   Long Down
6   Stoke Down
7   Nore Down
8   Easton Down
9   Martin's Clump
10 Durrington
11 Grime's Graves
12 Buckenham Toft
13 Den of Boddam
14 Skelmuir Hill
15 Ballygalley Hill

Northern
Province

Transitional
Province

Southern Province

land over 200.0 m

chalk

1
Introduction

Neolithic flint mines represent some of the earliest earthworks surviving in the modern landscape and provide the first evidence for large-scale extraction of stone or minerals in England. As archaeological sites they received some of the earliest antiquarian investigation, but despite this there has been little attempt to consider them as a class nationally, and some are known now only from obscure articles or unpublished archival sources. Many have never been surveyed or accurately planned. Consequently it was considered that a programme of surveys incorporating analytical field survey, aerial photographic transcription and archival research would help to meet the growing needs of site managers and conservationists, academic study and the informed reader. This project is particularly apposite since very few sites now survive as earthworks and even some of the partly levelled or cropmark sites still suffer from unsympathetic land use. The archaeological literature suggests an apparently extensive distribution of flint mines, but many of the references have been found to be illusory or incorrect, thus emphasising their overall rarity (Figure 1.1). This suggests that as a monument class flint mines urgently require a higher priority in the management debate if the remaining sites are to survive.

In contrast to previous research, this project has brought a 'landscape' perspective to the study, integrating the results of detailed fieldwork with documentary and archival sources to produce a more complete picture of site development, the context of the mines and their locational positions. This has allowed the opportunity of taking research beyond site-based subterranean studies, tool typologies, or the statistical analysis of the extraction process and to place flint mines into a wider contemporary context. In so doing weight has been lent to earlier suggestions that flint mines had affinities with certain other site types of the Neolithic period such as long barrows, causewayed enclosures, cursus and henge monuments. The evidence from the new earthwork surveys suggests that the scale of extraction at the mines was not intensive in a modern industrial sense. The mines were carefully located to the extent

that they did not always follow the better quality flint seams and were relatively small in size. They produced a range of cores and artefact types among which were products such as axes and discoidal knives. Like many other forms of Neolithic sites they contained placed deposits and graffiti, implying that flint mines had a role in the Neolithic period beyond the purely functional procurement of raw materials. It is interesting to note that many of these features occur in the mines of the earlier Neolithic in the South Downs and Wessex, and with some modifications re-occur in the later Neolithic period in the Breckland mines.

During the course of the project sixty-four sites were identified in the National Monuments Record, the relevant County Sites and Monuments Records, museum archives and the archaeological literature, of which fifty were visited. Forty-four were subsequently rejected as Neolithic flint mines; eight sites had a significant degree of uncertainty regarding their classification; two further sites had strong evidence to suggest that they were probably Neolithic flint mines; thus leaving only ten sites for which there was definite evidence for Neolithic flint mining activity. Undoubtedly new sites will be discovered, perhaps through the detailed examination of aerial photographic archives or relict woodland.

Sites were discredited for a variety of reasons. A number, such as Ringland, Drayton, or Cranwich, occur in the literature as a result of the identification of concentrations of 'industrial' flint debitage, but such debris does not of itself confirm the presence of Neolithic mining. Others were noted as a result of reports of tunnels and chambers found in the chalk, sometimes with deer horn (antler) present; however, antler merely indicates the use of a primitive tool which may have had a currency far beyond the Neolithic period. More importantly, the discovery of chambers such as those at the Lavant Caves in West Sussex (*see* McCann 1997), almost certainly indicates chalk extraction rather than flint. Vast quantities of chalk were used from the Roman period onwards for building purposes and for marling, for pipe clay or chimney

Figure 1.1 A distribution map of Neolithic flint mines in England showing their position in relation to the major chalk deposits. The Scottish and Irish sites are shown for completeness.

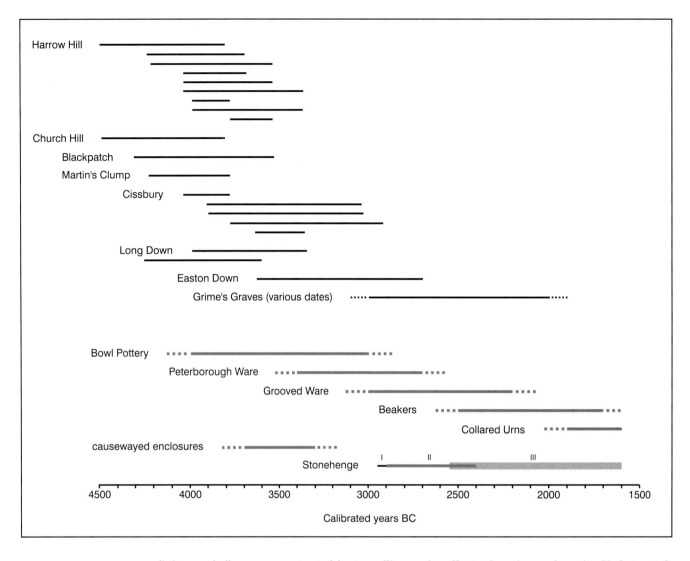

linings – chalk was even extracted by tunnelling within the urban areas of Norwich (Atkin 1983) and Thetford (Bruce-Mitford 1952). In the past this led to confusion among antiquaries, particularly in the late 19th and early 20th centuries when almost any denehole or natural 'swallow' hole was considered a potential flint mine.

Field investigation led to the rejection of certain sites traditionally accepted as flint mines. Great Massingham in Norfolk is an example, where marl pits occupy almost every field around the village, causing some ambiguity over the correct classification of the extraction sites. The shallow hollows noted by Plowright (1891) are situated upon a sand formation and are almost certainly the location of ironstone quarrying; even the gravel quarry site located upon the valley floor is without any evidence to confirm mining activity. However, there are locations in Massingham where concentrations of struck flakes are found close to the valley floors in positions where nodules gather naturally as a result of

the effects of erosion and gravity. Unfortunately the presence of struck flakes alone does not necessarily imply mining.

At Windover Hill, in East Sussex, field inspection showed that the depressions formerly identified as flint mines (see Curwen 1928; Holden 1974) invariably have access ramps for wheeled traffic. The so-called Roman trackway and road that ascend the downland escarpment appear to be integral to these quarries, suggesting that they are more likely to be medieval or post-medieval features associated with the construction or repair of Wilmington Priory, which is located at the foot of the escarpment. Flint was certainly being extracted there in 1853 when the diggers reported finding an Iron Age terret on the hilltop (Figg 1853, 259). Pitstone Hill, in Buckinghamshire, also appears to have been worked in the post-medieval period, while most of the depressions noted by Peake (1913) at Peppard Common in Oxfordshire, seem to represent surface grubbing for brickearth.

In contrast, sites were accepted as flint mines where excavation had confirmed their existence. The juxtaposition of distinctive earthworks (or cropmarks) associated with knapping debris were taken as evidence of probable flint mining (*see* Gazetteer). 'Presumed' sites consisting simply of surface debris were not considered to be mines but rather knapping sites or other forms of activity areas. The potential confusion with gun-flint mines is not an issue as the earthworks of the two site types are generally different in structure or associations (*see* Figure 3.1), and in most cases the gunflint mines are well documented.

Only ten sites fulfilled the criteria (Figure 1.1): Easton Down and Durrington in Wiltshire; Martin's Clump in Hampshire; Blackpatch, Church Hill, Cissbury, Harrow Hill, Long Down and Stoke Down in West Sussex; and Grime's Graves in Norfolk. Two additional sites with reasonable evidence to suggest they were also mines are Nore Down in West Sussex (partly confirmed by excavation; Aldsworth 1979; 1983) and Buckenham Toft in Norfolk (the presence of knapping debris adjacent to a shaft).

Those flint mines that have traditionally been considered destroyed, proved to be some of the more surprising sites. Slight earthworks were found to survive at Blackpatch and were recorded both by ground survey and aerial transcription to create as complete a plan as possible. At Church Hill the ephemeral, but still visible, earthwork traces of the mine complex – currently still under the plough – were also recorded by ground survey to preserve the surviving evidence by record before it is lost. However, the site at Stoke Down is now almost completely levelled and could only be recorded from the air, although the transcription has increased its size considerably to the extent that the complex now appears to follow the flint seam for a distance of some 750 m. The site at Durrington lies beneath housing development and is now beyond the reach of field survey and aerial photography. As a contrast, one of the few partly surviving post-medieval gunflint sites at Lingheath Farm, Brandon in Suffolk, was also surveyed (*see* Figure 3.1; NMR number TL 78 NE 81). This provided a well-documented example of a method of flint extraction which could be used for comparative purposes with the prehistoric sites. The gunflint sites are also of considerable importance in their own right as monuments to a vanished industry.

During the course of archival research much unpublished material was encountered, including artefact assemblages, for example antler picks from known contexts from earlier excavations. In partnership with the British Museum a suite of five radiocarbon assays was processed using some of these, producing new dates for Martin's Clump (1), Cissbury (2) and Harrow Hill (2) (Figure 1.2; Appendix 2). These dates broadly confirm the traditional view that the South Downs and Wessex groups were exploited during the earlier Neolithic period. These sites contrast with Grime's Graves which is firmly placed within a later Neolithic horizon, not only by the extensive radiocarbon chronology but also by the links between later Neolithic ceramics and the extraction process (Longworth *et al* 1988, 13). A synthesis of the chronology of the English flint mines is presented in Figure 1.2.

Earlier studies of flint mines (eg Sieveking 1979; Mercer 1981a; 1981b) assessed important practical aspects of mining, the technology, the processes of extraction, the quantities of raw material extracted, and so forth, while the British Museum study is also considering the utilitarian aspects of the mines. The present assessment steers a rather different course in order to investigate wider aspects of these sites and not only to contribute but also to broaden the debate.

The sites were surveyed using terrestrial analytical techniques aided by use of Electronic Distance Measuring (EDMs) equipment and Global Positioning Systems (GPS). The aerial transcriptions were digitised using a Digicart computer with AERIAL 4.2 software (published by the University of Bradford) from aerial photography incorporating 1940s Ministry of Defence verticals (when many of the sites were still earthworks) alongside those of the Ordnance Survey taken during the 1970s. These various approaches allowed the creation of a range of surveys sophisticated enough to map the slightest earthworks through the use of conventional hachures at most sites and terrain modelling using KeyTERRA-FIRMA software at Grime's Graves (Figure 4.15). This project has produced a corpus of large-scale plans (at 1:1000 or 1:500 scale) providing a national overview at a consistently high standard which should be an invaluable aid for future academic study and site management.

This book provides a synthesis of current knowledge up to December 1997. Comprehensive archive reports giving full details of all sites investigated during the course of the project, including those discredited, have been lodged in the National Monuments Record which can be contacted through:

National Monuments Record Enquiry and
    Research Services,
National Monuments Record Centre,
Great Western Village,
Kemble Drive, Swindon, Wiltshire SN2 2GZ.

Telephone: 01793 414600
Fax: 01793 414606
Web site: http://www.english-heritage.org.uk

Figure 1.2 (opposite) Synthesis of the chronology of English flint mines.

Despite the number of radiocarbon dates available for flint mines in England, the problems outlined on p 16 make it impossible to draw all but the most general conclusions. Grime's Graves is the best dated, and mining there seems to belong wholly to the 3rd millennium BC. At present, it is chronologically distinct from the other sites that have yielded any dating evidence. Excavations at several of these other sites have produced evidence for similarly late activity associated with Beakers, Collared Urns and Grooved Ware, but the radiocarbon dates derived from mining contexts are consistently earlier. They cluster around the first half of the 4th millennium BC, with hints that mining may have begun prior to 4000 BC at some, and continued well beyond 3500 BC at others. However, in the main, these are dates obtained around thirty years ago, they are of uncertain accuracy and precision, they possess substantial error ranges, and some are derived from charcoal samples. The newly obtained dates offer greater accuracy and precision, but still leave many questions unresolved. The number of dates is few when set against the size and complexity of the mines. Also worth highlighting is the fact that flint mining in England may have lasted 2,000 years or more. Set against the number of known shafts, each site may have seen the excavation of no more than a single shaft per year.

2
Previous research

Early investigations

The knowledge that prehistoric flint mining occurred in Britain dates from the publication of Canon Greenwell's incomplete excavation of a deep galleried shaft at Grime's Graves, Norfolk, between 1868 and 1870 (Greenwell 1870). Although by no means the first episode of excavation at a site now known to be a flint mine, this was the first occasion in this country on which the real date and purpose of such a site became apparent. Greenwell's visit to Grime's Graves occurred during a period of significant developments within the emerging discipline of prehistoric archaeology. The works of Lyell (1863), Lubbock (1865) and others had helped to establish the idea of a pre-Roman past of considerable, albeit unknown, duration. In addition, Thomsen's 'Three-Age System' of Stone, Bronze and Iron Ages, which provided an outline technological and chronological framework for this prehistoric period, had finally gained a firm foothold among British antiquarians and archaeologists.

Although dissenting voices remained (eg Wright 1885, vi–viii), the 'new' concepts and terminology were now replacing earlier approaches to the remnants of the past, which had drawn largely from the vague accounts of classical authors. The numerous and varied earthworks which dotted the countryside had been ascribed more often than not to historically attested peoples such as the Romans, Saxons or Danes, while pre-Roman Britain had been viewed as the realm of the Celts or Ancient Britons. The surface traces of prehistoric flint mines had not escaped such treatment, though their unusual nature allowed for a range of interpretations. Blomefield (1739, 148) described Grime's Graves as 'a very curious Danish encampment' (Figure 2.1), while Turner (1850, 181) suggested that the hollows in and around Cissbury hillfort, West Sussex might be '"dish barrows" – those "holy consecrated recesses" … formed for the special purpose of forwarding the celebration of the religious ceremonies of the ancient Britons during their sojourn in these hillforts'.

The first known excavations at these places did little to further knowledge of their nature and origins. Pettigrew (1853) and Manning (1855; 1872) both described episodes of shallow trenching within hollows at Grime's Graves in February 1852. To Pettigrew the site had evidently been 'formerly a seat of war between the Saxons and the Danes', whereas Manning believed that 'The place is, in fact, a British stronghold – a fortified settlement of the Iceni; probably of a date anterior to the arrival of the Romans' (1872, 171). Meanwhile, at Cissbury in 1856, Irving investigated a number of the hollows inside the hillfort, but appears to have committed a similar error as some later and more illustrious visitors to the site in failing to recognise the true depth of these features. Instead he speculated that the apparently shallow depressions might represent cattle enclosures or pig pounds (Irving 1857, 294). He regarded the hillfort as belonging to the Roman period on the basis of the few recognisable artefacts recovered (ibid, 283).

A significant step forward occurred a little over a decade later when Colonel Lane Fox (later known as Lieutenant-General Pitt Rivers) arrived at Cissbury, excavating some thirty of the hollows in September 1867 and January 1868, with Canon Greenwell present during the latter campaign. At the time, Lane Fox was pursuing a programme of research into the hillforts of the Sussex Downs, and had been struck by the quantity of worked flint scattered about the surface at Cissbury. He decided to dig

> in order to determine whether the
> indications of the stone age observable on
> the surface corresponded with those of
> the implements found in the soil; and if
> so, whether the positions in which these
> implements were found were such as to
> afford evidence of their having belonged
> to the people who constructed these forts
> (Lane Fox 1869b, 54).

Cissbury represented Lane Fox's first major excavation and, although the published presentation

Grime's Graves

of the results inevitably fell short of the standards he was later to achieve, his interest in attempting to understand the nature of the site rather than simply recover artefacts is clear (Bowden 1991, 70–1). He concluded at this stage that the depressions and hillfort were likely to be contemporary, though he flirted briefly with the notion that the latter might be later. His familiarity with lithic material led him to the conclusion that most of the artefacts recovered were likely to belong wholly to the Stone Age. As for the purpose of the pits, despite repeating Irving's error in mistaking their chalk rubble infill for the natural chalk bedrock, and thus failing to recognise their true depth, the quantity of nodular and worked flint recovered enabled him to propose that they had been dug 'for the purpose of obtaining flints' (Lane Fox 1869b, 73). However, there are indications that Lane Fox's intellectual path to this conclusion was not as straightforward as his excavation report suggests. In an earlier paper on

the Sussex hillforts (Lane Fox 1869a), read to the Society of Antiquaries of London after the excavations had ended, he commented that the Cissbury hollows might represent the sites of 'rude huts'. He made a similar claim for the hollows at Wolstonbury, West Sussex, though these actually represented the remains of post-medieval flint extraction, an error rectified in a footnote (Lane Fox 1869a, 41). There must be a possibility that the receipt of information concerning Wolstonbury prompted a rethink on Cissbury.

In later years, after the existence of deep and galleried shafts at Cissbury had been demonstrated by others, Lane Fox elaborated further on his first excavations there (Lane Fox 1876; Pitt Rivers 1884). He noted that flint seams at nearby Broadwater could be observed at depths of 3–6 ft (0.9 m–1.8 m), and thus considered that even his incomplete excavations had proved the Cissbury depressions to be deep enough to permit flint extraction, though he never claimed to have

Figure 2.1 The earliest known depiction of an English flint mine: a charcoal and pencil drawing of Grime's Graves in c 1850 by the Revd G V Luke of Weeting, Norfolk, showing the depressions covered by small trees. By courtesy of the Norfolk Record Office, PD 312/27. (BB96/5697)

Figure 2.2 A large abandoned flint nodule in gallery III²b at Greenwell's Pit, Grime's Graves. The gallery was excavated above the flint seam and the nodules prised up from the floor. (AA95/5161)

observed a flint seam in any of them. He also gave Canon Greenwell's involvement in the excavations a higher profile, effectively sharing the 'credit' for misinterpreting the chalk infill as the bottom of the pits. However, having correctly identified their purpose, Lane Fox claimed that he had 'left it for others to discover the extent of the pits and galleries branching from them' (Lane Fox 1876, 361).

Greenwell and Grime's Graves

Of course, the extent of the pits and galleries were first discovered not at Cissbury but by Canon Greenwell at Grime's Graves. Greenwell himself provided no clear explanation of how he came to be excavating there in 1868, though Pitt Rivers later suggested that the main stimulus had come from the discoveries at Spiennes, Belgium, the first major account of which had only recently been published (Briart *et al* 1868). Subsequently,

Canon Greenwell happening to be carrying on his excavations near Brandon, which has always been the great workshop of the gunflint manufactory, chanced to come upon a collection of pits similar to those of Spiennes and Cissbury ... and he decided to excavate them, in order to determine whether they also had shafts and galleries like the Spiennes pits (Pitt Rivers 1884, 70).

The rather impromptu nature, as implied by Pitt Rivers, of what turned into a fairly major undertaking is evident not only from Greenwell's account of the work (1870), but also from the re-excavation of the same shaft and all of its galleries a little over a century later (Longworth and Varndell 1996).

Between 1868 and 1870 Greenwell oversaw the excavation of a single shaft on the eastern side of the mine to a depth of 39 ft (12 m), reaching the bottom but not removing all of its infill. In the process, a series of what Greenwell (1870, 425)

referred to as galleries radiating out from the shaft's base were uncovered and partially explored. These galleries had been dug by the miners in order to exploit the preferred horizontal seam of flint, the so-called 'floorstone' layer (Figure 2.2). In digging down to reach it, the miners had cut through two other seams, the uppermost known as 'topstone' and the middle one as 'wallstone'. The terminology had been borrowed by Greenwell from the gunflint industry at nearby Brandon. Finds from the shaft and galleries included some struck flints plus various items of worked chalk. Some of the latter were interpreted as cups or lamps, while others had purposes of a less obviously practical nature, such as 'a representation of the glans of a human penis', which Greenwell compared with inferior modern graffiti (Greenwell 1870, 430–1). Mining tools were represented by numerous antler picks. Greenwell's most contentious discovery was of a ground axe made of epidiorite or greenstone (Clough and Cummins 1988, 47; Clough and Green 1972, 133), apparently found in close association with some antler picks within a gallery which bore traces of the axe's blade upon its chalk walls (Figure 2.3). In terms of contemporary understanding of prehistory, this discovery provided one of the strongest indications of a Neolithic date for flint mining at Grime's Graves, and as a result was a focus of attention during the later debate over flint mining chronology.

Greenwell's work at Grime's Graves inevitably prompted renewed excavation at Cissbury. Willett, who seems to have undertaken some unsuccessful digging at nearby Church Hill a few years previously (Law 1927), examined a galleried shaft at Cissbury in the autumn of 1873, following a suggestion made to him by Greenwell that a deeper search of the Cissbury depressions might be worthwhile (Willett 1875, 338). Willett noted that, as at Grime's Graves, the miners had ignored flint at a shallower depth in preference to deeper but presumably superior material. He also speculated that some of the galleries visible at the base of the shaft might join up with neighbouring shafts, something which was to be demonstrated clearly during later excavations at this and most other sites.

In January 1874, a further shaft at Cissbury was excavated by Tindall. Although he died shortly afterwards, an account of this shaft was included by Willett in his paper (1875, 341), the reading of which to the Society of Antiquaries of London prompted Lane Fox to return to the site and resume excavation (ibid, 347). Lane Fox's work recommenced in 1875 and continued until 1878 under the supervision of Harrison (Lane Fox 1876; Harrison 1877a; 1877b; 1878). Lane Fox's main concern in 1875 was with the relative

age of the flint mines and hillfort, something touched on by Willett and unresolved by Lane Fox's earlier investigation. Lane Fox and Harrison were able to demonstrate clearly that the mines were earlier, observing an infilled shaft which had been cut through during the digging of the hillfort ditch, as well as locating others sealed beneath the hillfort's rampart (Figures 2.4 and 2.5). Further shafts and their associated gallery systems both inside and outside the hillfort were investigated. Two shafts were found to contain human skeletons, one being that of a woman buried head down near the bottom of a shaft's infill. The lithic artefacts discovered strengthened Lane Fox's belief that the mines belonged to the Neolithic, though he noted a resemblance between some items and Palaeolithic forms. The presence of the remains of domesticated fauna as well as sherds of coarse pottery provided Lane Fox with important supporting evidence for a Neolithic date. Another noteworthy discovery was the presence of scratched or incised markings on the chalk walls of some shafts and

Figure 2.3 Impact marks made by a ground stone axe on the walls of gallery III[1] of Greenwell's Pit, Grime's Graves. (AA95/5162)

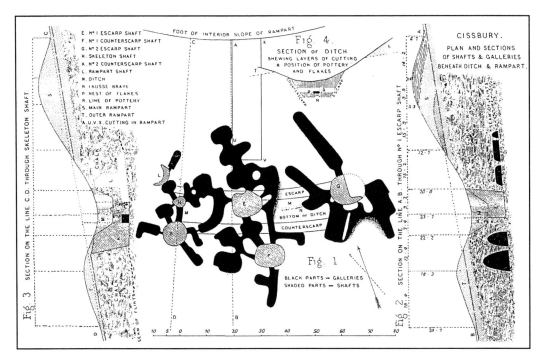

Figure 2.4 A plan by Colonel Lane Fox – later Lieutenant-General Pitt Rivers – of the 1875 excavations at Cissbury, which provided the first clear demonstration that flint mining preceded hillfort construction (Lane Fox 1876).

galleries (Figure 5.11). Harrison in particular became a little sidetracked with these, indulging in speculation as to their possible origin and meaning (eg Harrison 1877a), whereas Lane Fox and others were rather more sceptical.

After Lane Fox and Harrison had departed Cissbury, no further excavations of any real significance were undertaken at an English flint mine until Major Wade's examination of three shafts at Stoke Down, West Sussex between 1910 and 1913 (Wade 1922). Sporadic surface collection and perhaps some unrecorded digging appears to have continued at both Grime's Graves and Cissbury. A few more possible sites were identified, though exploration of these tended to be minimal at best (*see* Gazetteer). For example, in the late 1880s Plowright recorded some discoveries in a quarry pit at Great Massingham, Norfolk, which suggested the possible existence of a prehistoric flint mine or quarry there (Plowright 1891). Collyer conducted some poorly documented trenching within several hollows on Harrow Hill, West Sussex, though once again the true depth of these features appears to have eluded the excavator (Curwen and Curwen 1926, 105). A possible mine site at High Wycombe, Buckinghamshire, was revealed during the construction of a railway cutting *c* 1902, but there appears to have been no follow-up investigation (Anon 1902, 323). In addition, a few false identifications were made as archaeologists struggled to come to terms with marl pits and deneholes, two prime examples being those at Crayford (Spurrell 1880; 1881, 401) and St Peter's, Isle of Thanet (Lane Fox 1869c; Lane Fox *in* Greenwell 1870, 439), both in Kent.

Palaeolithic flint mining?

Renewed interest and excavation were stimulated by the publication in 1912 of a paper by Reginald Smith, then Keeper of British and Medieval Antiquities at the British Museum, in which he argued that both Cissbury and Grime's Graves were Palaeolithic rather than Neolithic in date. Despite Smith's use of the word 'revolutionary' (1912, 109), the suggestion that some of the flint artefacts from both sites closely resembled accepted Palaeolithic forms was hardly new. It had surfaced intermittently ever since the first excavations had been published, and both Lane Fox and Greenwell had discussed such similarities, albeit briefly. However, support for placing both of the excavated flint mines and their products within the earlier period had been growing for a number of years, with Greenwell's ground axe from Grime's Graves proving a notable stumbling block. As an accepted type-fossil of the Neolithic, it presented an obvious difficulty to advocates of the earlier dating. By the early years of the 20th century, doubts were being cast on its authenticity, doubts which were seemingly laid to rest by Sturge (1908) who went as far as to conduct enquiries in the Grime's Graves area as well as soliciting a further and more detailed account of the axe's discovery from Greenwell. Although the issue had effectively been settled, Smith took the opportunity to remind his readers that the rumours had existed (1912, 10, 117, 147, etc).

However, by 1912 the ground axe was a secondary issue. The whole problem centred upon contemporary understanding of prehistoric lithic technology and on the concept of the Neolithic. The term had been introduced by Lubbock in 1865 to describe the later of the two phases into which he felt the Stone Age was divisible. Characteristic criteria were, initially, few in number, though this reflected Lubbock's primary concern with technological progress as an indicator of human social evolution. Thus for a short while it was the production of ground stone axes which provided the principal distinction between the Palaeolithic and the Neolithic. Subsequent consideration and excavation permitted additional criteria to be confirmed, such as pottery, certain types of burial monuments, and the exploitation of domesticated plants and animals (*see* Thomas 1993 for a discussion of the changing content and meaning of the Neolithic since Lubbock).

The novelty of Lubbock's 'New Stone Age' is evident in the caution shown by Lane Fox in his first Cissbury report (1869b, 64). Greenwell (1870, 434) displayed more confidence in the concept, citing the presence of a ground stone axe and the bones of domesticated animals as reasons for assigning Grime's Graves to the

Neolithic. However, as already mentioned, both Lane Fox and Greenwell were already drawing attention to similarities between some of their flints and others of Palaeolithic form. Some four decades later, it was this same misunderstanding of lithic technology which was central to Smith's arguments. Working debris, roughouts and crudely flaked implements from the mines were directly compared with objects from Palaeolithic sites. The idea that some of these flint mine artefacts represented the early stages of implement manufacture rather than finished objects was rejected. In addition, the emphasis placed by Smith on the flints effectively reduced the importance to his case of more troublesome elements of the debate. Pottery, domesticated fauna and ground axes were claimed to present no problem to a Palaeolithic date once the argument over lithic typology had been accepted. He also sought alleged Palaeolithic occurrences of each of these artefact categories. The matter rumbled on into the 1920s, and a number of individuals were quick to point out the flaws in his argument, including Toms, who conducted his own flint

Figure 2.5 Colonel Lane Fox's excavations at Cissbury showing the upper lip of a mine shaft revealed in the base of the hillfort ditch. This view of 1875 is the earliest photograph of a Neolithic flint mine, and indeed of an excavated archaeological section. Reproduced by courtesy of the Sussex Archaeological Society.

knapping experiments in order to demonstrate how a 'Cissbury'-type Neolithic axe (*see* Figure 2.6) could be produced by working down an apparently Palaeolithic ovate 'hand axe' (*Worthing Herald Magazine*, 16 June 1923; Bradley 1989, 32–3). Some sites, such as Peppard Common, Oxfordshire, had already been published as Palaeolithic mines (Peake 1913; 1914). By the time Clark and Piggott published their paper 'The Age of the British Flint Mines' in 1933, there were few remaining who were willing to argue against a Neolithic date for these sites. However, Armstrong (*see* below) continued to put up some opposition, and a degree of uncertainty seems to have lingered in some quarters (for example Kendrick and Hawkes 1932, 74–5).

Grime's Graves 1914–39

The appearance of Smith's paper in 1912 prompted numerous articles on various aspects of the debate to appear over the next decade or so. Of greater long-term importance was the fact that it led directly to renewed excavations at Grime's Graves, and indirectly to the recognition and exploration of other important sites between the wars. At Grime's Graves, two galleried shafts and a number of surface working floors were examined in 1914 under the auspices of the Prehistoric Society of East Anglia (Clarke 1915b). The aim was to recover information with which to evaluate Smith's arguments, but the involvement of a number of the leading protagonists in the debate, including Smith himself, ensured an inconclusive outcome and made further work at the site inevitable.

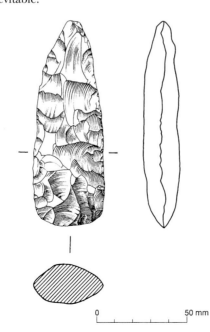

Figure 2.6 Following the excavations at Cissbury in the 1870s, 'Cissbury'-type axe-heads were often quoted as a type fossil. These were generally small flaked flint axes, with an asymmetrical plan and narrow or pointed butt, and even miniature versions occur (Field 1982; Gardiner 1987). Most appear to have been made on flakes, and it may be that such axes were transported some distances to other locations before grinding.

0   50 mm

Excavations occurred at Grime's Graves almost every year until the outbreak of the Second World War. Some of the individuals involved were genuinely concerned with investigating the problems concerning site chronology and function, though in retrospect a fair amount of the surface exploration, much of which is poorly recorded if at all, appears to have been little more than glorified flint collecting. It was the work of Armstrong that provided the most important results. An early supporter of the Palaeolithic dating, he had been involved in the 1914 excavations and was responsible for the first published survey of the site (Clarke 1915b, fig 1). He returned the following year to take part in further excavations, and subsequently he rarely missed a season's digging over the next twenty-five years. From 1920, his excavations became more ambitious as he sought to determine the full spatial extent of the mines and to develop a chronological sequence for mining at Grime's Graves, in the process clearing out several pits and shafts, and conducting extensive trial trenching away from the visible earthworks. As the clear evidence for Neolithic mining became increasingly apparent, Armstrong developed a phasing for the site which saw flint extraction originating during the Palaeolithic, represented by the simplest, ungalleried (or 'primitive') pits, and continuing on into the Neolithic. The deeper and interconnecting galleried shafts were assigned to this later period, reflecting a perceived development in the complexity of mining techniques over time (Armstrong 1927; 1934a; 1934b). When Clark and Piggott (1933) published their refutation of the idea of Palaeolithic flint mining, Armstrong (1934b, 384) firmly rejected their arguments, and continued to excavate further shafts at Grime's Graves for several more years, although he was never to publish much of this later work himself (*see* Longworth *et al* 1991; Longworth and Varndell 1996).

In his final year at the site, 1939, Armstrong was responsible for perhaps the most notorious discovery at Grime's Graves, the so-called goddess (Figure 5.9b), a carved chalk figure which, along with other objects, was found at the foot of Shaft 15. In an echo of the earlier ground axe controversy, the authenticity of this particular find has been open to question for a number of years. This was not the first time that Armstrong's excavations had yielded something of uncertain antiquity at Grime's Graves. In 1921 he reported on the discovery of some flint flakes which featured engraved or incised designs on their cortex (Armstrong 1921). Some of these images were apparently 'formless' but a few appeared to represent animals. Both Armstrong and Smith enthusiastically regarded these examples of prehistoric 'art' as further evidence for Palaeolithic activity at the

Figure 2.7 John Pull excavating in a gallery at Cissbury. Pull excavated two shafts here between 1952 and 1955, but due to his tragic death in 1961, the results were never published. By courtesy of Mrs M Suckling. (BB94/50050)

site, something which may have helped to promote doubts about their authenticity. The status of these objects remains uncertain at best. They seldom figure in any discussion of the site, although they do not represent the only incised images, formless or otherwise, to be reported from English flint mines.

The South Downs and Wessex 1922–55

While the work of Armstrong and others turned Grime's Graves into the most explored and best known of the English flint mines, a considerable amount of activity occurred at a number of important sites on the chalklands of southern England. Between 1922 and 1955, all three of Cissbury's near neighbours in the Worthing–Findon area of West Sussex, Blackpatch, Church Hill and Harrow Hill, as well as Cissbury itself, were subject to campaigns of excavation which in the cases of Blackpatch and Church Hill were of quite lengthy duration. Meanwhile, in the late 1920s, the known distribution of flint mines was expanded westwards following the discovery and excavation of the site at Easton Down, Wiltshire, by J F S Stone, who was also responsible for the identification of a further site nearby at Martin's Clump, Hampshire, a few years later.

Easton Down and Harrow Hill are relatively well known, reports of the various excavations undertaken at each site having appeared fairly promptly in archaeological journals, although neither site can be regarded as unproblematic. The situation regarding Blackpatch, Church Hill

and Cissbury is rather more complex. All three were investigated by John Pull (Figure 2.7), a Worthing-based Post Office worker who, though largely self-taught as an archaeologist, conducted his excavations to what were relatively high standards for the time. Unfortunately, much of his work remains poorly known today because of a difficult relationship with members of the local archaeological 'establishment' in Sussex (White 1995; *see* Russell forthcoming).

Pull had first encountered the site at Blackpatch, West Sussex in 1922, and began to excavate the same year with assistance from his colleague Sainsbury. Further help was soon forthcoming from the recently established Worthing Archaeological Society, among whose more notable members were Elliot and Cecil Curwen, who via their fieldwork and publications were later to make important contributions to archaeology both locally and nationally. Pull's own report on the 1922 season was rejected by a committee of the Society, which instead published its own account in the journal of the Sussex Archaeological Society (Goodman *et al* 1924). Pull resigned from the Worthing Archaeological Society in protest, and along with several colleagues he publicly disassociated himself from the published report, most notably in a letter to the *Worthing Herald* in which he stated his

> admiration for the editorial committee in
> producing the undoubted work of art,
> especially considering the artistic manner
> with which it ignored all necessary and no
> doubt troublesome data.

The most immediate result of this dispute was that the Worthing Archaeological Society moved on to Harrow Hill in order to investigate the flint mines there. Pull remained at Blackpatch for the rest of the decade, before moving onto Church Hill (1932–52, though interrupted by the Second World War) and finally Cissbury (1952–5). Of greater significance was the fact that the dispute led Pull to turn to alternative local outlets such as the *Worthing Herald* and the *Sussex County Magazine* in order to publish his work. Although they often contained considerable detail, the contents of these numerous articles inevitably escaped the attention of many of his contemporaries as well as subsequent generations of archaeologists. In 1961, having retired from the Post Office, Pull was shot and killed in a bank raid while working as a security guard. His sudden death prevented the preparation of any full account of his numerous investigations on the Downs, which were by no means confined to the flint mines. His best-known publication remains his book *The Flint Miners of Blackpatch* (Pull 1932), written for a general audience rather than an academic one, and omitting much of the detail contained within his newspaper articles and notes. Unfortunately, this point was overlooked by some of those who dismissed it at the time. For example, Clark and Piggott, who had first met each other in 1928 while working on Cecil Curwen's excavations at the Trundle, West Sussex (Piggott 1983, 30), claimed that while Blackpatch 'must have yielded most valuable evidence it is presented so unscientifically that we cannot utilize it' (Clark and Piggott 1933, 183; *see* Pye 1968 and Russell forthcoming for details of Pull's excavations).

The lack of awareness of Pull's work is particularly unfortunate given the nature of his discoveries and the extent of his excavations. At Blackpatch, he examined eight shafts, most of which proved to have galleries, plus four working floors. In addition he investigated twelve features which he described as round barrows, although re-examination of his published notes and archives suggests a more complex situation with implications for both the chronology of the site, and the association of funerary and ceremonial activity with the mines. Further shallow circular features away from the mines and described by Pull as possible 'dwellings' belonging to the miners are more difficult to evaluate. At Church Hill, the excavations again focused on the mine shafts but also examined other features including round barrows and a circular enclosure (Figure 2.8). Discoveries particularly worthy of note from Church Hill included fragments of a possible wooden vessel, possible traces of a ladder, and the presence of further markings or 'pictograms' incised into the chalk in some of the galleries of one shaft. At Cissbury,

where just a couple of shafts and working floors were investigated, four further images resembling animal heads were found carved into the chalk on gallery walls (Holgate 1991, 32; Pull archive, Worthing Museum & Art Gallery).

Of the Worthing group of mines, only Harrow Hill was not investigated by Pull, although as noted above it did not escape the attention of the Worthing Archaeological Society, who conducted excavations on two separate occasions. The first, led by the Curwens in 1924 and 1925, involved earthwork survey as well as the investigation of a single shaft (Curwen and Curwen 1926). Three flint seams were encountered, and all proved to have been exploited to varying degrees. The uppermost had been subjected to some opencast quarrying; the middle seam had been worked via two galleries and some opencast extraction; and the third and lowest was exploited via a series of galleries radiating out from the base of the shaft. Again, incised markings on the chalk walls supplemented the usual finds of antler picks, bone tools and flint flakes. Further excavations in 1936 were led by Holleyman and focused more on the enigmatic later prehistoric enclosure which overlaps the mined area. Inevitably mine shafts were encountered and three were examined, one of them lying beneath the bank of the enclosure (Holleyman 1937).

Easton Down, Wiltshire, was another site at which more than just the mine shafts were examined (Stone 1931a; 1931b; 1933a; 1933b; 1935). Stone had initially been drawn to the area because of an observed convergence of linear earthworks in the immediate vicinity. Between 1930 and 1934 Stone examined half a dozen shafts and several working floors, as well as a round barrow, a series of Collared Urn-associated cremations concealed beneath a low cairn of flint nodules, and various pits and arrangements of stake-holes. Perhaps the best known of the latter was a collection of stake-holes and furrows interpreted as the remains of a rectangular building of later Neolithic/Beaker date, although the precise form, interpretation and date of the structure remain a matter for debate (Darvill 1996, 81, 107). As for the mine shafts, most lacked galleries, though there were instances of shallow undercutting at the base. In some cases, no flint seam was encountered at the bottom of the shaft, and Stone interpreted these as having been left unfinished.

Grime's Graves – renewed investigations

After Armstrong completed his final season in 1939, no excavation occurred at Grime's Graves until 1971–2, when the need to display the site satisfactorily and safely prompted the examination

Figure 2.8. (opposite) John Pull's plan of the Church Hill flint mines showing the results of various excavation campaigns. Reproduced by courtesy of Mrs B Heryet and Worthing Museum & Art Gallery.

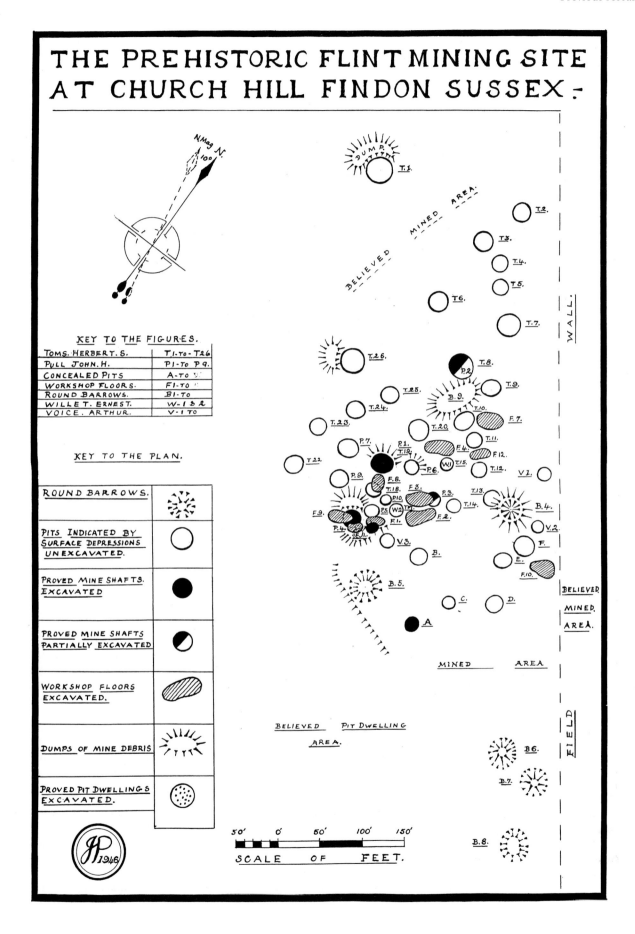

THE PREHISTORIC FLINT MINING SITE AT CHURCH HILL FINDON SUSSEX.

KEY TO THE FIGURES.

TOMS. HERBERT.S.	T.1-TO-T26
PULL JOHN.H.	P1-TO P9
CONCEALED PITS	A-TO ?
WORKSHOP FLOORS.	F1-TO ?
ROUND BARROWS.	B1-TO ?
WILLET. ERNEST.	W-1 & 2
VOICE. ARTHUR.	V-1 TO ?

KEY TO THE PLAN.

ROUND BARROWS.	
PITS INDICATED BY SURFACE DEPRESSIONS UNEXCAVATED.	
PROVED MINE SHAFTS. EXCAVATED	
PROVED MINE SHAFTS PARTIALLY EXCAVATED	
WORKSHOP FLOORS EXCAVATED.	
DUMPS OF MINE DEBRIS	
PROVED PIT DWELLINGS EXCAVATED.	

JP 1946

50' 0' 50' 100' 150'

SCALE OF FEET.

of another galleried shaft and the area surrounding it, with a view to opening it to the public. The primary aims of these excavations, directed by Roger Mercer on behalf of the Department of the Environment, were to glean as much environmental, cultural and chronological information relating to the period of mining as possible. A secondary aim was to examine traces of any Bronze Age activity at the site. Armstrong had encountered a considerable quantity of mid- to late Bronze Age artefacts and associated debris, notably in an area christened 'the Black Hole', but the nature of this later activity had remained obscure. The evidence obtained by Mercer comprised a substantial midden deposit within the upper fill of a second shaft which was partially examined in 1972. A further, similar deposit was excavated during the subsequent research excavations undertaken by the British Museum and led by Gale de G Sieveking. The site has now produced a considerable quantity of Deverel-Rimbury and later pottery, as well as broadly contemporary lithic, bronze, and bronze-working assemblages.

The British Museum programme, which ran from 1972 to 1976, involved geophysical and contour surveys of the site, as well as the excavation of several opencast and shallow pits, plus a number of flint working areas. In addition, Greenwell's Pit and four other previously excavated shafts were cleared out and surveyed with the assistance of members of the Prehistoric Flintmines Working Group of the Dutch Geological Society, Limburg Section, led by P J Felder. In conjunction with Mercer's excavations, the British Museum campaign and its resulting series of publications have ensured that Grime's Graves remains the best explored and best known of the British flint mines (*see* Mercer 1981a; 1981b; Clutton-Brock 1984; Longworth *et al* 1988; 1991; Legge 1992; Longworth and Varndell 1996).

The South Downs and Wessex – 1955 to the present

Since Pull, the discovery and exploration of flint mines on the southern chalk has been more sporadic and less intensive in nature. A number of sites have been claimed as flint mines, though few have seen sufficient excavation to yield positive evidence in support of the identification. One of the confirmed sites is Long Down, West Sussex, which was investigated by Pull's colleague, Salisbury, between 1955 and 1958 (Salisbury 1961). More problematic are sites such as those at Nore Down, West Sussex (Aldsworth 1983) (Figure 4.10), Slonk Hill, East Sussex (Hartridge 1978, 87), and Windover Hill, East Sussex (Holden 1974), all of which have seen extremely

limited excavation. In the case of Windover Hill, the field survey suggests that the earthworks represent flint and chalk quarrying of a rather more recent date. A little further afield, six shallow pits revealed at Durrington, Wiltshire, during the cutting of a pipeline in 1952 represent exploitation of a shallow seam of flint (Booth and Stone 1952). Stone's earlier identification of Martin's Clump, Hampshire, as a flint mine has been confirmed by some poorly recorded excavations carried out in 1954–5 by a Colonel Watson from nearby Porton Down (Ride and James 1989) and by more recent observations from the digging of a pipe trench (Ride 1998).

More meaningful survey and excavation occurred at a number of the Sussex sites during the 1980s. In 1982 and 1984, Sieveking, partly in conjunction with Felder and his Dutch colleagues, excavated a shaft at Harrow Hill, along with some surface working areas and some smaller pits (McNabb *et al* 1996). Between 1984 and 1986, Holgate carried out a plough damage assessment of the Sussex mines on behalf of English Heritage. As well as surface collection and ground survey at Church Hill, Long Down, Harrow Hill and Stoke Down, he also undertook geophysical survey and sample excavations at Long Down and Harrow Hill. At Long Down a surface flint working area was excavated and three shafts partially examined, while at Harrow Hill a flint working area and several opencast pits were explored (Holgate 1989; 1995b; 1995c; Holgate and Butler forthcoming).

Flint mines and the British Neolithic

Understanding of the British Neolithic was transformed in the wake of discoveries at causewayed enclosures and other sites during the 1920s and 1930s. It was material from sites such as Windmill Hill, Wiltshire, and Whitehawk, East Sussex, which enabled Clark and Piggott (1933) to argue so persuasively in favour of a Neolithic date for the flint mines. This expansion of the empirical evidence also provided the basis for new surveys of the period, culminating in Piggott's seminal publication *Neolithic Cultures of the British Isles* (1954). However, subsequent discoveries and a diverse range of theoretical approaches have left little of Piggott's interpretative framework untouched. While the Neolithic continues to be viewed as a period which saw the introduction of new forms of subsistence, settlement, funerary ritual, material culture and so on, the spatial and temporal unity implicit within a culture-historical framework of the sort followed by Piggott has been increasingly broken down.

The introduction of agriculture and correspondingly more settled lifestyles have long been viewed as pre-conditions for the various social, economic and cultural achievements of Neolithic societies. Among the more notable of these are the construction of various forms of monuments, and the widespread dispersal of certain artefact categories, both central to many discussions of social and economic organisation during the period. Reappraisal of the empirical and theoretical basis for the view that the Neolithic was primarily founded on fundamental changes in the nature of food production has led to a willingness to assign a prominent role to indigenous Mesolithic groups in bringing about the changes observed in the archaeological record. Furthermore these changes, particularly in regard to subsistence and the appearance of less mobile lifestyles, are now considered to have been far more gradual than previously allowed (eg Thomas 1993; Whittle 1996).

Where does this leave the flint mines? From the 1930s onwards, their Neolithic credentials established, they were seen as the source of the flint axe (Figure 2.9). They represented the large-scale and specialised production of an essential tool, which was manufactured and traded by full-time craftsmen and used in the establishment and maintenance of agricultural communities within forest clearances. However, while it is evident that flint mine products were used for purely practical tasks, it is now also clear that extraction of raw material was by no means the sole function of, or activity at, flint mines. The products of those mines could, and did serve more than utilitarian functions.

These are issues which have been examined in more detail with regard to objects, principally axes, made from types of rock other than flint, these having proved more susceptible to petrological examination. Early discoveries such as the 'axe-factory' site at Graig Lwyd (Warren 1919) helped to promote a belief that these other raw materials also derived from specific locations, analogous to flint mines, at which the rock was quarried and preparatory working undertaken. Such a philosophy has underlined much of the work on implement petrology now carried out under the aegis of the Council for British Archaeology, but whose origins lay in curiosity over the source of the Stonehenge bluestones and in the presence of stone artefacts and fragments of non-local material in the ditches at Windmill Hill, Wiltshire (Grimes 1979). The resulting attempts to group artefacts by rock type and to identify a source for each had specifically excluded flint, the nature of which posed particular difficulties for this style of scientific examination. Likewise, attempts to interpret the observed distributions of axes of particular grouped rocks have tended to overlook the presence of significant quantities of flint axes in the archaeological record. Attempts to characterise flint implements and sources began at a much later date (*see* for example, Sieveking *et al* 1972; Craddock *et al* 1983; Bush and Sieveking 1986) but have yet to yield satisfactory results (Figure 2.9) (Gardiner 1990; Pitts 1996, 17–18).

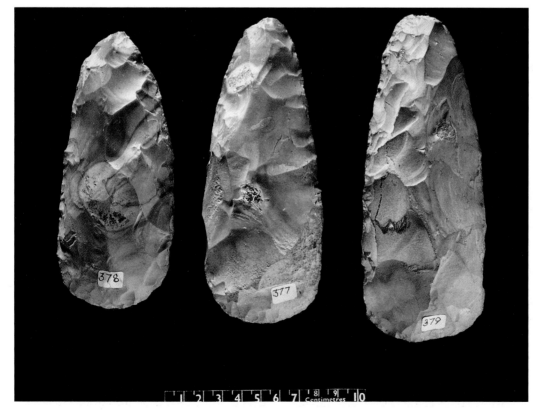

Figure 2.9 Hoard of flaked flint 'Cissbury'-type axes from Peaslake in Surrey (Bruce-Mitford 1938). These were included as samples in the British Museum programme of analysing trace elements to determine the source of the material (Craddock et al 1983) and were considered to be made of material derived from the South Downs.
© Copyright The British Museum.

Both the flint and non-flint characterisation programmes have been subject to similar criticisms. The problems with the implement petrology programme have been raised on numerous occasions, notably by Briggs (1976; 1989) and Pitts (1996), but perhaps most effectively by Berridge (1994). The main difficulty stems from the fact that neither the so-called stone axe factories nor the flint mines represent the sole potential source of raw material for axe (and other implement) manufacture in prehistory. The recognised 'stone' sources occur over wide areas both as natural outcrops and secondary deposits including glacial erratics, while usable flint is similarly accessible in southern and eastern England from Clay-with-flints deposits, from surface outcrops, and over wide areas of the British Isles from secondary deposits. Non-mine sources of flint, such as the outcrops at Flamborough Head, East Yorkshire (Sheppard 1920; Manby 1979; 1988; Durden 1995; 1996) and Beer Head, Devon (Powell 1920; Woods 1925; 1929), have long been recognised. More recently, however, the difficulties experienced in identifying flint mine products among excavated assemblages and surface collections have served to highlight the problems involved in understanding the role of flint mines, particularly when one considers the enormous quantities of flint estimated to have been extracted from them (Mercer 1981a, 112–13; Healy 1991; Longworth and Varndell 1996, 85–9). The existence of non-mine sources, clearly utilised during the Neolithic, raises the issue of why mine shafts were dug at all. The view that mines should be regarded as centres for the production and distribution of tools and other items made from the best quality flint resembles the ideas and assumptions applied to the so-called 'axe factory' sites and the implement petrology programme discussed above. But recent work at places such as Great Langdale, Cumbria (Bradley and Edmonds 1993), has clearly demonstrated that neither the best quality, nor the most easily extracted material was being quarried and utilised for tool production. This further emphasises the close relationship between social, cultural and technological choices likely to have existed during the Neolithic.

Problems also surround flint mine chronology. Piggott's (1954) short chronology for the Neolithic helped to support the idea of intensive exploitation and specialisation. However, much of what Piggott crammed into the period 2000–1500 BC is now more spaciously accommodated within the 4th and 3rd millennia BC. Radiocarbon dates are available from most of the excavated mines (Figure 1.2; Appendix 2). The work undertaken by Mercer and Sieveking at Grime's Graves during the 1970s yielded a considerable number of dates for the site, in addition to further determinations from material previously recovered by Armstrong and Greenwell. These indicate clearly that mining at Grime's Graves, at least in those areas excavated and dated, occurred almost wholly within the 3rd millennium BC. In contrast, a much smaller series of dates obtained from other flint mines, using material excavated by Harrison, Pull, Stone and others, appears to suggest that the Sussex mines were in use much earlier, during the early to mid-4th millennium BC, with Easton Down a little later in date. However, these radiocarbon determinations are not without their problems. For many of the sites there is only a single date, and given the size of some of the mining complexes this is hardly adequate. Furthermore, the reservations expressed recently about some of the Grime's Graves dates (Ambers 1996) may well apply to the Sussex and Easton Down dates, obtained as part of the same dating programme, using artefacts from early excavations and uncertain contexts. In an attempt to gauge the reliability of the existing determinations, further samples were submitted for radiocarbon dating during the course of this project. The results are shown, together with the existing dates, in Figure 1.2 and their implications discussed below in Chapter 5. The problems surrounding chronology are further underlined by the excavated evidence from sites such as Blackpatch, West Sussex and Easton Down, Wiltshire. Here, burials associated with Beakers and Collared Urns were recovered from the area of the mine shafts, indicating that the sites were a focus for activity in the late 3rd or early 2nd millennium BC, though it is unclear if any flint extraction was continuing at such a late stage. At nearby Church Hill, the presence of Grooved Ware and Beaker sherds is equally noteworthy.

That uncertainty still surrounds such fundamental issues after 130 years of archaeological research relating to flint mines and their products may seem surprising. To a considerable extent these uncertainties result from the discoveries and new theoretical and interpretative perspectives of more recent years. However, the variable quality of the extant evidence from the excavated mines and the quantity of unpublished data are also significant factors that limit the potential for the creation of adequate interpretative frameworks.

3
The use, nature and location of the raw material

The use of flint: a historical perspective

For over half a million years flint was probably the most important raw material to be utilised by hominids within the British Isles. Perhaps the best example of the early use of flint is from Boxgrove, West Sussex, where scores of bifacially flaked flint tools were found adjacent to butchered animal bones at the foot of a chalk cliff. The site is now known to be some half a million years old (Roberts *et al* 1994), demonstrating the longevity and importance of this hard, sharp stone. At Boxgrove the raw material may have been obtained from rockfalls or the cliff face, but there is also evidence that bifaces were made elsewhere and brought to the site, while at other Palaeolithic sites such as Hilton and Willington in Derbyshire (Posnansky 1963), flint was being collected and carried for considerable distances from the chalk.

During the final 'Devensian' glaciation in the Upper Palaeolithic period (*c* 35,000–8000 BC) a more economical method of using flint became widespread. This involved the manufacture of large numbers of flint blades for cutting purposes struck from a single nodule, rather than relying upon large tools such as hand axes. Although there is as yet no evidence in Britain for the quarrying of raw material at this time and although secondary deposits could have been used, the finds from sites such as Hengistbury Head, Dorset (Barton 1992), or sites in the Severn and Wye Valleys (artefacts in Gloucester Museum), all suggest that the nearest chalk – in this case the Wiltshire Downs – was providing surface flint. Within Britain there is no evidence for the use of large flint tools at this time and the introduction of axes, adzes and picks may have been influenced by Scandinavian or eastern European prototypes early in the Mesolithic period (Field 1989, 1). Many of these tools discovered along the Thames Valley were made from large gravel pebbles (ibid, 2), but even upon such secondary deposits of flint there is no unequivocal evidence of quarrying. However, the so-called 'dwelling pit' at Farnham could alternatively be interpreted as a quarry for gravel

flint (Ellaby 1987, 67), and the large numbers of picks made of Portland Chert found on the Isle of Portland might imply some local extraction. Similar flint picks and associated crude tools – the material formerly referred to as 'Campignian' and thought to represent discarded mining material (Gabel 1957, 92) – have been found in large numbers on the deposits of Clay-with-flints in Surrey, Hampshire and Dorset, and might represent evidence for 'grubbing' up flint nodules (Care 1979).

The grinding of axes, an innovation perhaps introduced late in the Mesolithic period but generally attributed to the Neolithic, rounded off awkward flake scars and made the finished tool more durable. The earliest date for a ground axe from a Neolithic context was recorded at the Sweet Track in Somerset, dated by dendrochronology to 3807/3806 BC (Hillam *et al* 1990, 218).

Fundamental to the need to mine for flint is the nature of its flaking properties. While surface-derived raw material can be used to make many forms of artefacts adequately, the flaws caused by frost damage make such material unpredictable to knap. However, exploiting mined flint from some depth not only resolves this problem but also offers the additional advantage in that greater control can be exercised over the flaking process. Each seam generally provides flint with different characteristics offering some choice to the knapper. The distinctive seam of black flint at Brandon, Suffolk, known as the 'floorstone' was prized by the British Army during recent centuries for its quality of sparking repeatedly – a vital feature for a flint-lock musket. However, its aesthetic qualities were also considered important, and consequently, piles of flint extracted by the gunflint miners were covered with bracken to prevent them from drying out and developing a 'milky' patination. Although the 'milky' flint was perfectly usable, buyers would only purchase black flints and a small trade developed in 'blacking over' grey blemishes (Skertchley 1879, 25; Forrest 1983, 85). During prehistory these differing properties were almost certainly recognised, and there are many examples of stone axes that appear to have been made for aesthetic value rather than as functional tools (eg Whittle 1995, 254, fig 4).

The use of flint in prehistory, however, was not confined to tool making. Flint 'potboilers', or stones used for heating water, and crushed flint used as filler in pottery fabrics are frequently encountered on archaeological sites. In addition there is some evidence of an early use of flint for construction. Features sealed within long barrow mounds on Salisbury Plain, for example, often comprised a platform of flint nodules upon which bodies were laid out, and over which a ridged or circular cairn of flint, or earth and flint, was constructed (Hoare 1810, 21). These flint nodules may have been recovered from surface deposits, but more likely were quarried from a local source, possibly the long barrow ditches themselves.

The impact of the early use of copper does not appear to have affected directly the need for good flint. Indeed, radiocarbon dates for the extraction of flint at Grime's Graves (Ambers 1996), and for copper extraction on Ross Island, Ireland (O'Brien 1995), overlap to some degree. This is all the more intriguing given suggestions that the flint from Grime's Graves may have been used primarily for prestige objects (Healy 1991, 35). Although flint daggers and barbed and tanged arrowheads represent some of the finest flint knapping seen in prehistory, it is precisely these items that might be expected to be among the first produced in copper. Radiocarbon dates suggest that copper was introduced into Britain at about 2500 BC, and that metal was subsequently used for about five hundred years during a period traditionally thought of as the later Neolithic (Needham 1996, 123). Eventually, however, flint technology did change, as weaponry, tools, and ritual and ceremonial artefacts were made in bronze. Other rocks continued to be quarried for maceheads and hammers (Smith 1979), and it is conceivable that flint was too. Flint certainly continued to be utilised, and nodules were in some cases collected for the construction of funeral monuments, for example the Bronze Age mounds in Micheldever Wood, Hampshire (Fasham 1979), or those at Blackpatch, West Sussex (Pull and Sainsbury 1928; Pull 1932). One Bronze Age barrow at Burpham, West Sussex, comprised some 183 tonnes of flint and stood to a height of 1 m at its centre (Curwen and Curwen 1922, 16–20). A second, at Brighton, subsequently reused for road metalling was even larger and said to have comprised roughly 305 tonnes of flint (Griffith 1924, 260).

During the Iron Age and Romano-British periods flint continued to be used for construction but on a massive scale. Tons of flint were required to construct the enormous 3 m high plinth for the monumental arch at Richborough; flint was used for the construction of Roman town walls and buildings at many southern towns such as Chichester (eg Down 1993, 105); for roads and villas (eg Williams 1971, 170) and for the forts of the Saxon Shore (eg Johnson 1976, 37–9). Nodules for the town walls and amphitheatre at Silchester are thought to have been dug directly from the local chalk (Sellwood 1984, 224; Blagg 1990, 39), and the location of Chichester close to the South Downs may have led to quarrying into the nearby chalk. The reputed Neolithic flint mines on Bow Hill, West Sussex (Hamilton 1933), overlie an earlier trackway, and it may be that these depressions represent the site of Roman or medieval extraction.

Throughout the medieval and post-medieval periods flint continued to have a wide range of uses, being built into the walls of churches, cathedrals, castles, and town walls, and also used for road metalling (see Passmore 1903, 264; Curwen 1930, 237–9; Passmore 1943, 52–3). Some of the material may have been collected from beaches, but mined flint was certainly prepared for building stone at Brandon during the 19th century (Skertchley 1879, 34–6). It is thought too, that the extensive quarries and tunnels in chalk at Norwich (Atkin 1983; Ayers 1990; Harris 1990, 207–8; Kelly 1994) and elsewhere represent the mining of flint for similar purposes. The shaft at East Horsley in Surrey, originally thought to be Neolithic, may also be an example of this (Wood 1952). Chalk rock was also extensively mined for building purposes (Bruce-Mitford 1952) and it may be that many of the early reports of presumed Neolithic flint mines, for example the Lavant Caves in West Sussex or Warlingham in Surrey, were the sites of much later chalk extraction. The depressions on Windover Hill, East Sussex, traditionally assigned to the Neolithic period (eg Thomas 1997, 300–1), more readily fit this later horizon, perhaps providing both flint and chalk for the construction of Wilmington Priory located at the foot of the escarpment.

During the 17th century there was a flourishing trade in flint for glassmaking (Mason 1978, 26–7). Skertchley noted (1879, 37) that calcined flint was reintroduced in the manufacture of china in order to whiten it, and during the 18th century enormous quantities of flint, mostly from beaches, were shipped to Stoke-on-Trent for that purpose.

Flint, however, has had other uses, principally as Skertchley noted (1879, 36) for 'strike-a-lights' which have been used throughout history. Skertchley recorded details of the 'old-English' strike-a-light, with its retouched horseshoe form resembling prehistoric scrapers, which heralded the development of early gunflints. Surprisingly, although flintlock muskets were introduced to the English Army about 1686, the mass production of gunflints did not begin until some twenty-five years later (ibid, 3) and continued until the introduction of percussion caps in 1835. Skertchley noted that a 'good flint will last a gunner about half a day', and in his own experiment fired a pistol with a gunflint 100 times, recording that it fired 36 times, flashed 25 times and misfired on 39 occasions (ibid, 4). The sparking qualities were of paramount importance to the military and many manufacturers gained or lost contracts because of this.

Little is known of the extraction processes at many of the gunflint centres. At some, flint was extracted from seams close to the surface or was produced as a by-product of chalk quarrying; at others such as Broad Chalke in Wiltshire, shallow pits were dug to obtain the raw material (Clay 1925a, 423), while at Beer Head in Devon it may have been extracted directly from the sea cliffs. The best-documented site is that at Brandon in Suffolk (Figures 3.1 and 3.2), where Skertchley (1879, 5–15) described not only the mines themselves, but also the elaborate geometric method of extracting the flint (ibid, 21–7) (Figure 3.3) that provides a useful insight into mining and provides contrast with the methods of the Neolithic miners. He noted that some miners preferred to sink a shaft close to trees as the chalk was drier, and he also described how the proximity of old workings was avoided because of the possibility that the extent of earlier 'burrows' might impinge upon the new pit, although when exceptionally good stone was extracted new shafts were occasionally sunk among the old. When shafts were sunk near to each other in summer and the air was 'stale', workings were linked underground in order to create a draught.

> … The shaft is begun by digging a trench three yards long, one yard wide, and one yard deep. The long sides generally run N and S … at one end of this an opening is made and carried down to a depth of five feet, slightly inclining towards the eastern side of the original trench. The shaft is carried down another five feet, and a staging left on the western short side, and so on to the floorstone, the front and right sides having no stagings. The shaft is only sufficiently large to admit a man, and it inclines … so as to undercut about two yards in 30 feet … the object of this is to prevent any stones falling from the upper stages … The floorstone is pierced to a depth of about 6 inches and then a gallery or 'burrow' is carried slantingly under the stone.

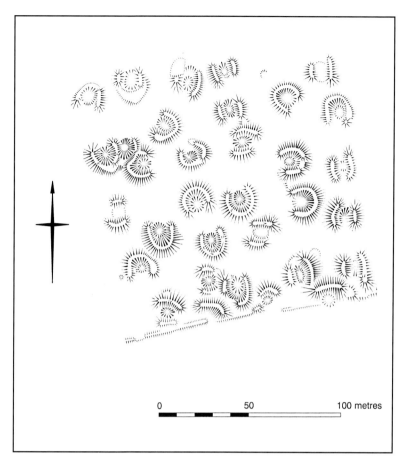

Figure 3.3 shows the method pursued in extracting the 'floorstone'.

The first main burrow A is entered through an orifice 18 inches high and two feet wide, the floor of which slopes downward for about 3 feet, the roof (from which the stone has been removed) being nearly horizontal. The main burrow is about 2 yards wide and is driven straight for about 9 yards, and the chalk and stone carried to the surface. At the end of this burrow a 'draw' (1) is made; that is, the workman lying on his elbow picks away the flint from above as far as he can reach, thus forming a semi-circular space about 18 inches high; this he continues, and, if the stone be good, he will draw 3 yards in each direction. The stone and chalk from the first draw are carried to the surface. The chalk is always thrown to the head of the pit and the stone to the foot. A side burrow, a, is then commenced from near the beginning of the main burrow, and of the same dimensions. It is carried in a curvilinear direction so as to catch the end of the first main burrow. The chalk and stone are carried to the surface. About

Figure 3.1 The earthworks of the gunflint shafts at Lingheath Farm, Brandon in Suffolk. Note the spaces left in the spoil dumps where nodules could be placed by the miner, each facing towards a common route between the shafts. The spacing too, between the shafts has some regularity and is a result of marking out an area on the surface for each shaft.

Figure 3.2 The old town sign of Brandon, Suffolk, showing the silhouette of a gunflint knapper. (AA96/2814)

Figure 3.3 (opposite) Skertchley's diagram (1879) illustrating the methods of extraction employed by the gunflint miners of Brandon.

half-way down the side burrow the first drawing-burrow, (a), is then made of the same dimensions as the others, and the spaces (2) and (3) are drawn into the main burrow, the chalk and stone being carried out. From the end of the side burrow, (a), the space (4), is then drawn similarly to (1), but not to so great an extent. The second side burrow, (a1), is then made, and the second drawing burrow a1, and the spaces (5, 6 and 7), are drawn as above, the chalk and stone being carried out; thus leaving all the space between the two side burrows empty. The second main burrow B is then driven, and all repeated as above, but only the stone and large 'chalks' are carried out; the smaller pieces, or 'fine muck', being filled into the first main burrow. This second main burrow is, as are all the burrows, of the same dimensions as the first … When the side and drawing burrows are completed the space (12) is drawn from the second side burrow a and the 'fine muck' filled into (a). The space (13) is next drawn from side burrow (b) and cleared out as far as possible. Pillars are shown in the figure at the intersection

of the side burrows; these are, however, not often left, but the spaces J, J, J, J, are always left as pillars or 'jarms' to support the roof. The above process is repeated in all respects as shown in the figure, the 'fine muck' from main burrow C and its adjuncts being filled into B, … etc. When the floorstone is exhausted, the pit is generally filled in up to the level of the wallstone, which in consequence of its 'legs', is burrowed from above. A main burrow A is driven for about three yards and the chalk and stone carried out. The space (a) is then drawn, and the drawing right round as shown in (a, a1, and a2), the material being carried out. The second main burrow B is then made of the same size and length, and the chalk filled into A; C and D are then made in the same manner … The jarms J, J, J, J, are left as before. The pit is now filled up to the toppings, unless building stones are in great request when the Upper Crust is burrowed. The same method is adopted as in the case of the wallstone, but some times the stone is merely drawn round as far the workman can reach. After the Toppings

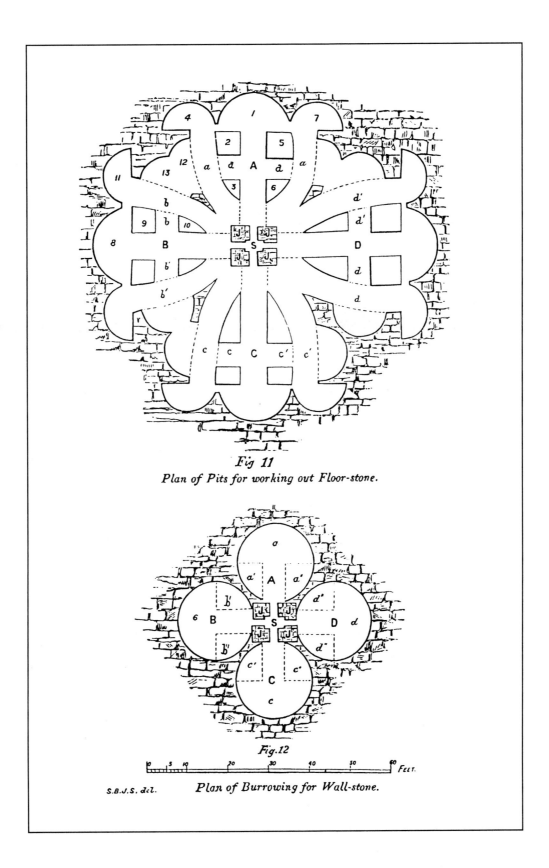

Fig 11
Plan of Pits for working out Floor-stone.

Fig.12

S.B.J.S. *del.* *Plan of Burrowing for Wall-stone.*

are got the pit is filled in, nearly to the surface … In the burrows the men sit and pick by the light of a candle but in the draws they have to lie sideways resting on their left arm and working with their right … The flint is brought up in pieces averaging 2 feet by 18 inches, and stacked edgeways on the ground around the pit's mouth. The stacks are covered with dried bracken and fir bough's to prevent the sun and wind getting access to the stone, and cracking them, or turning them milky in colour, for only black flint is used for the best gunflints, though the milky stone is equally as good. The merchants will buy only black flints … A good pit lasts from six to nine months. The burrows are never timbered, and accidents from falling roofs are rare.

Hewitt (1935, 20) noted that by the 1930s miners at Brandon no longer extracted 'floorstone' in the manner recorded by Skertchley during the previous century. Herbert Edwards recalled how the mining process was carried out up until the Second World War when 'Pony' Ashley, the last of the gunflint miners retired.

… In bringing up flint from their pits, the miners piled it in heaps to make 'jags' (measured by eye 1 jag = about 13 cwt). … start with an unbroken bit of heath … there with your tools, a pick, hammer and spade, you make your first cut, twelve feet by six feet. You then dig the soil out to the depth of your first staging, four foot six inches to five feet down. Most stagings are about that depth. Once there you cut out the centre, leaving a solid platform on three sides of the staging, and down you go, switching directions to the next level and so on stage by stage each at right angles to the previous one, until you strike 'floorstone' … once he gets to the … 'floorstone' level, the miner works his way along the seam of black flint. He burrows in straight lines, his directions so far as he could estimate north, south, east and west. Each burrow runs ten to twelve yards in 'gain' from the toe, its height from two foot six to three feet, and width at the bottom three to four feet … he would first raise his flint on to the staging nearest the toe; then with that stage loaded he sprang up, using footholds in the chalk, and lifted his flint on to the next staging and so on. It might take half a dozen lifts to reach the top. He carried heavy lumps on his head, raising them first chest high against a wall;

and then ducking underneath, he headed up his flint platform by platform (quoted from Forrest 1983, 18–22).

Although the techniques of gunflint mining were undoubtedly different from those of the Neolithic miners, the hard physical labour and the cramped and damp working conditions would have been very familiar.

One final and less obvious use for flint was as ballast for both ships and barges. Some of this flint, mainly derived from southern beaches, was off-loaded at northern docks such as Newcastle and Sunderland, where massive piles of ballast were held (Bird 1963, 45, 56, fig 11), but it was also dumped at sea and ultimately found its way onto beaches around the coast by the effects of wave action. Field inspection of flint found along the Northumberland coast suggests that most of it originated as ballast. Such ballast was also transported further afield, and Holland (1994, 4) recounts how English flint nodules were washed up on the coastline of Maine in North America, having been either deliberately off-loaded or washed from wrecked ships.

Geology

Flint itself is one of the hardest rocks occurring within the British Isles, registering second only to diamond on the mohr scale. In composition it consists of needle-like crystals of silica, with the occasional presence of Cretaceous sponge spicules and micro-fauna (Shepherd 1972, 34; Brooks 1989). The processes of formation are incompletely understood (*see* Shepherd 1972, 68–107 for an outline of the various theories), although recent work has shed considerable light on the matter (eg Bettermann *et al* nd, 26; Buurman nd, 23–5; Bush nd; Clayton 1986). In general terms, the marine sediments in which flint is found contain large quantities of silica and the origin of flint appears to result from the redistribution of this mineral.

In its natural state, flint occurs in an endless variety of shapes and forms, from the giant, hollow, barrel-like paramoudras (or sea pears), to worm-like coils and rings, and networks of branches that extend over considerable distances (Shepherd 1972, 21–2). It is more usual, however, to encounter it as tabular sheets and seams of irregularly shaped nodules. Although examples of vertical seams do occur, flint is usually bedded horizontally, or nearly so, each band featuring slightly different shades of grey ranging from almost white to black.

In the past visual inspection was used to assign a general provenance to flint, but this is quite problematic as flint taken from the chalk is remarkably uniform across the Cretaceous deposits in England. Experiments with dye have demonstrated that flint absorbs moisture at a remarkable rate (Patterson and Sollberger 1979, 50), and accordingly it soaks up minerals from its immediate surroundings. This perhaps helps to explain the variety of colours found in flint recovered from secondary deposits at a distance from the parent rock. However, coloration and patterning has its limits in England where no deposits of patterned flint are yet known to compare with those in Europe such as the striped (Borkowski and Budziszewski 1995) or chocolate-coloured flint of Poland, or the honey-coloured flint of Grand Pressigny, France. Arguably, one of the few genuinely distinctive deposits is the lustrous flint from the Bullhead Beds found at the junction of the chalk and overlying Tertiary deposits in the Thames Basin. This does have a distinguishing orange stain beneath a greenish-black cortex and is represented in many prehistoric flint tool assemblages discovered in this area.

The distribution of flint-bearing deposits in England

In England the distribution of flint is directly related to the former extent of the Cretaceous chalk (*see* Figure 1.1). Before the Pleistocene the chalk massif was considerably more widespread than at present, probably extending as far to the north-west as Chester, and erosion has resulted in widespread deposits of durable flint gravel at great distances from the present position of the chalk. In the west there are flint-based gravels in north-west Devon and south Wales (Jukes-Brown 1903, 2). Off-shore Cretaceous deposits in the outer part of the Bristol Channel and to the south of Beer Head in Devon (Barne *et al* 1996a, 20–2; 1996b, 24–5), may have resulted in nodules being washed up on beaches. In the south-east the chalk deposits extend beneath the English Channel into France where they form part of the Anglo-Paris basin, and, similarly, the chalk in Yorkshire and Lincolnshire extends beneath the North Sea towards Germany (Jukes-Brown 1900, 4; Mortimore 1982). Chalk exposures still exist on the sea bed off Flamborough Head and Scarborough in East and North Yorkshire respectively, and there are widespread flint gravel deposits off the coast of both Yorkshire and Lincolnshire, and south towards the Wash (Harrison, 1990, 6 and maps; Barne *et al* 1995, 22–5).

The English chalk, a very fine calcareous limestone, is the result of the deposition of sediment on the sea bed between 144 and 65 million years ago, and reaches a thickness of 1,000 m in places.

During the 19th century geologists divided these deposits into three units (Jukes-Brown 1903, 5): the Cenomanian, the Turonian and the Senonian, known more commonly as the Lower, Middle and Upper Chalk respectively. No flint is present in the Cenomanian and little in the Turonian, although its frequency increases in the higher levels. It is the Senonian or Upper Chalk deposits that are of most interest, being up to 300 m thick in places and containing abundant flint seams (Jukes-Brown 1900, 1–2). While this sequence has become embedded in archaeological literature as a result of excavations on the chalk in Sussex, it was based on geological studies of the southern chalk alone, and did not take account of the rather different characteristics of the northern chalk. Recently, the traditional three-part chronological classification has been superseded by one which divides the chalk into three regional Provinces (*see* Figure 1.1): the Northern, the 'Transitional' zone, and the Southern. Each of these is sub-divided into a series of Members, based on the nature of the chalk and flint seams within them (Mortimore and Wood 1986, 7). It is particularly important to note these regional differences as they contribute towards the discussion concerning the location of the mines and why they developed in some areas and not others. Refinement of this system, particularly in Dorset and Devon, may allow the prediction of areas of likely flint extraction. Where possible this classification is followed here.

The Northern Province

The chalk of the Northern Province in East Yorkshire and Lincolnshire has long been considered to be different from the southern chalks (Kendall 1907, 57). It is of greater density than that in the south, it is exceptionally hard and in places almost cement-like. As Kendall (1907, 61) noted, tools used to dig chalk in Kent will not suffice in Yorkshire, and it has been suggested that it is this hardness that prevented attempts at flint extraction in the north (eg Manby 1979, 71; 1988, 42). To further emphasise this difference, the macro-faunas within the Northern Province are considered to have greater similarities to those of Germany and Russia than southern England (Mortimore and Wood 1986, 8). Flint deposits occur only in the lower chalk rather than in the upper layers, and the flint itself is typically pale grey in colour and appears to splinter rather than fracture cleanly.

Mortimer (1878) noted that within Yorkshire, the chalk containing flint is only exposed at the surface some way inland in a narrow band to the west of Beaverthorpe, Fimber and Beverley. There is too, a very thin strip a little over 1 km wide, which curves eastwards to outcrop on the north side of Flamborough Head, the most southerly point of coastal outcropping being at the aptly named Silex Bay (Selwicks on the recent Ordnance Survey map). There is also the possibility of an off-shore source, where the chalk lying off Flamborough Head has been eroded (Harrison 1990) as the coastal zone of this area has changed considerably since the Neolithic (Manby 1988, 39).

Despite the difficulty of digging into such hard cement-like chalk, earthworks were in fact quite frequently constructed on this formation during prehistory. Apart from long barrow ditches, substantial pits were dug beneath certain barrows such as those at Aldro, which were 4.5 m and 3.6 m deep respectively, both cutting through layers of flint (Mortimer 1905, 53–82). At Duggleby Howe, a similar pit, 2.7 m deep, was covered by a mound, the superstructure of which comprised chalk rubble and stood to a height of up to 3.0 m (ibid, 24).

Although Sheppard (1920, 35–6) recognised the widespread presence of flint in Yorkshire, he noted that it was extremely brittle and easily shattered. He also made the point (presumably based upon visual analysis) that only 5 per cent of flint axes found in Yorkshire at that time seemed to have been made of Wolds flint. While it has been suggested that nodular flint has better flaking qualities than tabular, it appears that the seams that lie close to the surface have been affected by glacial activity and are thus less workable than material found at greater depth (Manby 1979, 71; 1988, 42; Henson 1985, 5). Despite the lack of evidence for extraction sites in Yorkshire, it has been suggested that raw material originating from Yorkshire was widely used further north, and is thought to have been transported as far as the Wear Valley (Young 1984, 7) and Cumbria (Durden 1996).

A similar picture emerges in Lincolnshire. Tabular flint from the Burnham Formation outcrops widely in areas of the north-east of the county, while nodular seams of the Welton Formation certainly appear to have been utilised as raw material for artefacts (Guirr et al 1989, 115; Phillips 1986, 89–94). However, Moore (1979, 85) claims that the flint axes recovered in the East Midlands are predominantly of glacially-derived flint, and instead cites the presence of nodules in the secondary deposits of the Trent gravels as the source of this raw material (Henson 1989). Like Yorkshire, the Lincolnshire flint is often considered too brittle for making axes. However, despite this, most of the flint axes found on the Wolds appear to be fashioned from chalk flint (Phillips 1989, 45). An assemblage recovered from Salmonby, which included axes and picks, was considered to comprise 50 per

cent chalk flint artefacts (Phillips et al 1990, 7–8), and it has been suggested that the quarry ditches of long barrows and other monuments may have provided the raw material from seams lying relatively close to the surface (Phillips 1989).

The Southern Province

In contrast, the chalk of the Southern Province is soft and the typically dark grey flint occurs in the upper rather than the lower levels. Gaster (1944) mapped the Sussex chalk using the traditional macro-fossil zones, illustrating where they outcrop, thus allowing some comparison of the relative positions of the mines, and this has been superseded only partly (Mortimore 1982, 32). While the British Geological Survey has retained the traditional tripartite division in the south for mapping purposes (Bristow et al 1997), many other subdivisions are now recognised and Mortimore's (1986a) detailed scheme for the Sussex chalk has been incorporated, with six Members, each divided into a number of Beds. This scheme has placed the flint mines at Cissbury and Church Hill within the first and second nodular seams of the Peacehaven Beds of the Newhaven Member, contrasting with Blackpatch and Harrow Hill where sheet flint seams lying between the Rottingdean and Old Nore Marls were exploited (Mortimore 1986b, 23). The use of poorer quality flint at the latter two quite prominently-located mining sites has profound implications on their interpretation, for better quality flint could easily have been obtained at other nearby locations. It would appear that the topographic position of these sites may have been more important than the quality of the raw material that was available at these locations.

The Transitional Zone

Lying between the two provinces, particularly around the Breckland of East Anglia, is a third 'Transitional Zone' (Mortimore and Wood 1986, 8). Here the chalk is similar to that of the Southern Province, but the bedding and in particular the flint, resembles that of the Northern Province. Included within this zone is an important sequence of flint seams referred to as the Brandon Flint Series, part of which, the 'floorstone', has figured prominently in archaeological literature. The nature of these seams is of some importance for the interpretation of mining at Grime's Graves.

The geological progression is still largely based on that of Skertchley (1879) who was able to observe the strata at first hand in the shafts of the gunflint miners at Brandon, and from this proposed a sequence across much of the Breckland area. The names applied to the various flint seams by the local miners were adopted by both

Skertchley and Greenwell, and as a result these have passed into general archaeological usage. Some seven seams of flint were recorded, and while any of these might be used for making artefacts, the Brandon gunflint knappers considered some impractical because of the size or shape of the nodules. In itself, the depth of the seam below ground appears to have been of little importance, as long as it was deep enough to avoid the effects of frost and periglacial activity. Skertchley's section (1879, 6 and fp 6; and *see* Hewitt 1935, 20) incorporated 'Horns' (small finger-shaped flints), 'Toppings' (knobbly on the upper side and flat underneath) and the 'Upper Crust' (round and lumpy nodules in a discontinuous seam and used for building stone), all lying above a continuous seam of 'Wallstone' (with 'pap' or knobs on the upper surface and horn-like projections called 'legs' below). This latter deposit was generally black, but sometimes grey or spotted, and was said to flake well with little waste. The 'Floorstone' lay beneath the 'Wallstone' and was distinguished by a continuous layer of dense black nodules up to 1 m wide, which had a thick white cortex. Very large masses of flint were often found below the floorstone and described by Skertchley as 'gret eggs' (sic), each of which was said to provide half a cartload of raw material. Other continuous seams also lay beneath the floorstone such as 'Gulls' and 'Rough and Smooth Blacks', which the Brandon miners considered to be the best for knapping purposes.

Devon

Beyond the three regional provinces the chalk of south Devon is perhaps the least investigated, and little work has been undertaken to establish a modern stratigraphic sequence. Deposits of chalk occur along the coast between Sidmouth and Lyme Regis (Rowe 1903), and inland for some 20 km (Edmonds *et al* 1975, 74; fig 18; Tingle 1998). Most of this is of the Turonian (Middle Chalk) series (Jarvis and Woodroof 1984), although it incorporates both tabular (sheet) flint and nodular seams in its upper levels. Outcrops of Senonian (Upper Chalk) with abundant flint seams occur in the sea cliffs on both sides of Beer Head, but little investigation has been undertaken upon them. Flint from some of these seams can be extracted easily, although deposits also accumulate on the beach from cliff falls. Knapping quality appears to vary considerably, but inspection confirms that at least one high-level seam consists of good black flawless flint. The effects of erosion make it impossible to determine whether collection from the beach and/or quarrying of the cliff face took place during the Neolithic period. In addition there is no surface trace of mining activity around the cliffs, although a 'Celtic' field system may have obscured any earlier earthworks which might have existed.

Secondary deposits

While the effects of glacial and periglacial activity and other prolonged periods of severe weathering have reduced the chalk cover to a fraction of its former extent, the processes involved have also ensured that the more durable flint which it contained has been widely redeposited. These secondary deposits are quite extensive and can be found in gravels occurring on high level plateaux, the terrace systems along many southern rivers (Gibbard 1986, 142), and coastal deposits around Southampton Water, the mouth of the Salisbury Avon, the Stour and the coastal fringe of East Anglia. Beaches, spits and off-shore deposits also produce extensive spreads of redistributed flint along coastal areas.

In the north, boulder clays containing flint nodules occur. Much of the chalk around Holderness, to the south of Flamborough Head, is covered by drift material, and Sheppard (1920, 35–6) pointed to these boulder clays as a source of raw material for flint implements found in East Yorkshire. Fieldwork by Manby confirmed that flint from the Boulder Clay is available on the beaches, and that many of the artefacts collected from the cliff tops around Flamborough Head are evidently of this material (Manby 1988). In addition he noted the presence of flint scatters around the heads of coombs leading down to the beach nearby.

In the south of the country parts of the higher chalklands, particularly the interfluves, bear a Clay-with-flints capping. The distribution of these deposits is particularly intense over parts of Devon, Dorset, Hampshire, the Chilterns, and the North Downs, and less so in Wiltshire and the South Downs (Catt 1986, 153). As a result of work in Sussex (Gardiner 1984) and Cranborne Chase (Barrett *et al* 1991) where Mesolithic and Neolithic activity was focused upon these areas, these deposits can be seen as increasingly important. The deposit is quite variable, however, ranging from heavy red clays in some areas, to silty clay loams in others, and has, at least in the archaeological literature, become a catch-all term for a complex of high level material that includes the remnants of the Blackheath, Woolwich and Reading Beds and other formations that often occur under the heading of Plateau Drift. Clay-with-flints *sensu stricto* is a stiff red clay with up to 50 per cent mostly fractured flint, but with occasional complete nodules found at the base of the deposit where they have escaped periglacial action (Loveday 1962, 86). In contrast, Clay-with-flints *sensu lato* is widely regarded as comprising a blend of parent material with greater or lesser proportions of clay, sand and flint pebbles derived from the overlying Reading Beds or allied formations. In Dorset, where remnants of the overlying London Clay and Reading Beds gradually diminish towards the west, the deposits of Clay-with-flints on Cranborne Chase are of this latter type and were a focus for late Neolithic activity (Catt 1986, 154; Fisher 1991, 11). Similarly, Neolithic sites on the North Downs in Surrey, when considered in detail, tend to occur on well-drained locations on isolated patches of sand and gravel overlying the chalk rather than on Clay-with-flints *sensu stricto* (Wood 1952; Field *et al* 1991, 144–5). The flint content of the deposit varies considerably in both density and nature, from unworn flint nodules to sub-angular fragments and pebbles, to areas where flint is completely absent. Catt (1986, 157) points out that most of the raw material, particularly from the Plateau drift deposits has been shattered, and while complete nodules exist at the base of the Clay-with-flints *sensu stricto*, these could only be obtained by digging through intractable clay or be found on valley slopes where the deposit outcrops, locations where better quality flint would be easily available from the chalk strata only metres away.

As has already been observed, the North Downs in Surrey and Kent, the Hampshire Downs and the chalk downland in Dorset all appear to lack flint mines. In contrast they are associated with dense spreads of Clay-with-flints. Care (1979) has suggested that with the exception of those from rivers, the density of axe distribution provides an indication of the locations of axe production and thus roughly the general source of the raw material. Care concluded that much of the material came from the Clay-with-flints that overlies the chalk in certain areas, and that these surface sources, first utilised during the Mesolithic, continued to be used during the Neolithic. Subsequent intensification in some areas may have led to the development of flint mines. However, although known flint mines lie close to such deposits, they are not primarily located in dense areas of Clay-with-flints. Conversely, as we have seen, some areas of dense Clay-with-flints, in Hampshire or the North Downs for example, have little evidence of mining. Throughout history there has been a general reluctance to cultivate the intractable Clay-with-flints in Surrey, Kent and Hampshire, and only latterly has this been attempted following the availability of modern farming machinery (Jones 1960), thus if any mines had originally been dug in these areas they should have survived into recent times.

Chert

While chert artefacts frequently occur in archaeological assemblages, for example from the Mesolithic sites in the Yarty Valley in Devon (Berridge 1985, 4–5), and even though the nature of sites investigated on the Isle of Portland (Palmer 1970) suggests local extraction, no quarry sites are presently known. Geologically there is no distinction between flint and chert, although the latter is generally identified by its greater density and coarser crystalline structure (Jukes-Brown 1900, 359, Betterman and Ackermand nd, 27). Chert beds are widespread, occurring in sandstones and limestones throughout Britain, often in the form of small nodules. However, chert distribution is not well mapped. In the north, sources occur around Weardale (Young 1984, 7), and in the limestone formations of the Pennines outcropping in Upper Ribblesdale, Wharfedale, Nidderdale and Swaledale (Manby 1979, 71). In the south, outcrops occur extensively in the Upper Greensand and are recorded from Dorset, Somerset, Devon, Wiltshire and the Isle of Wight. Like flint, chert also occurs in secondary deposits of gravels, at Golden Cap and Stonebarrow in Dorset, on the Blackdown Hills in Somerset and Halden Hill in Devon, for example (Jukes-Brown 1900, 191, 211, 218, 326); some of the nodules from the latter site were said to be large enough to use as building stone.

Distribution of the mines

In view of the extensive deposits of flint, the known distribution of Neolithic flint mines and quarries is comparatively restricted. Secondary deposits of gravel flint were certainly quarried in places as separate as the Den of Boddam in Scotland (Saville 1995, 353) and Rybniki in Poland (Borkowski *et al* 1995, 525–6). Consequently we might expect similar quarries in England, particularly in areas away from the main flint-bearing strata. However, there is no direct evidence for the quarrying of nodules from Clay-with-flints, boulder clay or secondary gravels, although these sources have been considered important and capable of producing flint of adequate quality for even large artefacts (Care 1979; Manby 1979; Gardiner 1984; Catt 1986). The implication is that these sources were exploited in an *ad hoc* way without a systematic approach through mining or quarrying.

Even on the chalk, mines are restricted to relatively few areas. Certainly it is conceivable that further sites await to be discovered, particularly in Wiltshire or Dorset where mines may have been confused with natural features or later quarrying. As a result, apart from a number of single unconfirmed and doubtful mine shafts on the North Downs, only three areas of mining activity can be identified at present: the Breckland group, located primarily in Norfolk, the Wessex group, lying on the Wiltshire/Hampshire border and the South Downs group.

The Breckland group

The principal site of the Breckland group is Grime's Graves, with a possible outlier nearby at Buckenham Toft. There is a series of further possible extraction sites ranged along the river valleys around Norwich, all inland from the Great Ouse/Wash catchment and perhaps associated with the Neolithic sites on the Fen edge. Grime's Graves also falls into this general pattern lying on a low interfluve between the Rivers Little Ouse and Wissey, which in turn feed into the Great Ouse/Wash. Capping the chalk of this latter site is boulder clay with cryoturbated chalk in the valley. A series of prominent periglacial soil stripes focus attention on a pingo on the valley floor, and it may be this striking juxtaposition of geological features which first attracted early visitors to Grime's Graves (*see* Figure 3.4).

Figure 3.4 An aerial view of Grime's Graves. The effects of periglacial action can be seen as stripes in the top right of the photograph. The concrete capping of Greenwell's Pit can be seen at the bottom of the photograph. (NMR 15769/10)

The Wessex group

This small group of extraction sites, Martin's Clump, Easton Down and Durrington, lies close to the Hampshire/Wiltshire border. None lie on the local deposits of Clay-with-flints, but all exploit shallow flint deposits – in some cases tabular flint seams actually form the ground surface. Both Martin's Clump and Easton Down lie on the interfluve above the tributary streams of the River Test, while Durrington lies on a bluff above the River Avon, high locations but not particularly dramatic ones.

South Downs group

In Sussex, the mines are centrally situated upon locally dramatic rolling downland; the smaller complexes in the west and the largest in the east. All sites lie on the Sussex White Chalk, close to, but not primarily on small deposits of Clay-with-flints that crown the hilltops. Some, such as Cissbury, Church Hill, and Long Down, lie on false crests just above dramatic slopes, and it may be that it was the erosion of these slopes that first pointed to the presence of workable flint seams. The presence of cappings of Clay-with-flints on some hilltops is important. Traditionally considered so intractable that it was not cultivated, it would support different vegetation from the chalk and thus be visibly different when viewed from a distance. In contrast to the chalk it is remarkably impervious and different rates of weathering can be expected at the interface, the chalk weathering faster. This, together with steep downland slopes, is likely to have promoted erosion and perhaps even the undercutting of the Clay-with-flints, effectively revealing flint seams at these points. Eroded flint would inevitably accumulate on the lower slopes and must have been an early source of collection, resulting in the presence of knapping sites at the foot of downland scarps such as Fairmile Bottom, Madehurst in Sussex. To the east of the River Ouse, the chalk contains no known mines, although much of the landscape, particularly around Beachy Head, has been eroded by the sea since the Neolithic period.

Survival and threats

The capacity of early farmers for clearing 'industrial' landscapes for cultivation is demonstrated at Cissbury where the shafts have been partly obscured by a system of 'Celtic' fields (Figures 3.5 and 3.6). Similar fields lay close to the mines at Harrow Hill and Blackpatch, and also encroached upon the mines at Easton Down. The extensive 'Celtic' field systems on Salisbury Plain where lynchets have developed to several metres in height could also have obscured other extraction sites. Indeed, the enormous 'Celtic' field scarps (the 'Walls') bordering the henge at Durrington suggest that any further mine shafts or pits nearby may have been obliterated at a relatively early date. Any trace of extraction on the summit of Brading Down on the Isle of Wight has been obscured by 'Celtic' fields, even though much debitage lies on the surface, while the field system on the cliffs at Beer Head could equally have hidden earlier mining activity. It may be that geophysical prospection could resolve these questions.

Other sites have been plough-damaged during the medieval and post-medieval periods. In Sussex, Long Down suffered from three separate episodes of cultivation (the earliest being prehistoric), and originally Nore Down may have been much more extensive, but is now partly hidden by strip lynchets. Easton Down and Martin's Clump have both suffered from post-medieval ploughing. According to Ratcliffe-Densham and Ratcliffe-Densham (1953, 69), Blackpatch was bulldozed at the request of the War Agricultural Committee, but Pull's pre-war records state that certain mine shafts were only identifiable by differential grass growth, suggesting that an earlier episode of ploughing had already reduced part of the site (Pull 1932). It is almost certain that further flint mines remain to be discovered, perhaps within woodland or the forestry plantations of the Breckland. The development of modern farm machinery has led to the clearance and 'improvement' of extensive areas, such as the gunflint mines at Lingheath Farm (Forrest 1983), and elsewhere massive sites comprising over 1,000 shafts of Neolithic date (eg Jablines, France) have been totally ploughed out (Bostyn and Lanchon 1995). Threats from modern cultivation continue at Church Hill and Stoke Down where ploughing still regularly occurs.

As the Lingheath example demonstrates, even in the sandy Breckland the flint mines have been affected by cultivation, and the central part of Grime's Graves has only survived partly because of an episode of tree planting during the 19th century and partly from the fact that it lay at the junction of three parish boundaries at a point furthest from adjacent villages. Even so, medieval 'breakland' cultivation had taken place in the West Field and to the south of the site obscuring at least one third of the mining complex. Additionally, sand blows such as that recorded in 1668 which buried houses at nearby Santon Downham (Suffolk Record Office: HD 1321/1), may have obscured other extraction sites in the Breckland. The little-known site at Buckenham Toft, for example, has been partly covered by a soft sand and subsequently levelled, perhaps during parkland landscaping, which may have hidden further elements of the site.

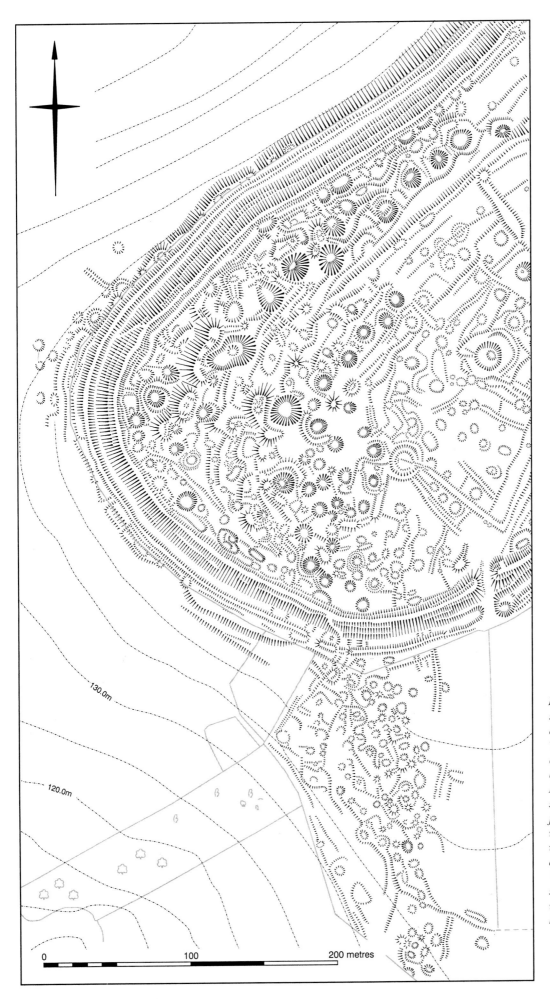

Figure 3.5 An earthwork survey of the flint mines at Cissbury, West Sussex. The Iron Age hillfort has created an artificial boundary to the mines. Parts of the complex can still be seen emerging from beneath the ramparts in the north-west and to the south-east. Note how the 'Celtic' fields have started to level the flint mine complex in the hillfort interior.

130.0m

120.0m

0   100   200 metres

Figure 3.6 An aerial view of the flint mines at Cissbury. Note how the shafts occur in rows along the contour of the hill. (NMR 1193/10)

Sites located elsewhere in England could have suffered a similar fate. Stoertz (1997, 3–6) records a pattern of cultivation on the Yorkshire chalk resembling that in the south, thus discoveries of earthwork sites are unlikely. Flint mines might be revealed by soil marks from the air, but the interpretation of such patterning is problematic and requires ground verification.

The growth of towns may also have concealed certain sites, particularly the expansion of London towards Northfleet in Kent, where gunflint manufacturing was recorded, and in Norwich, Thetford and Bury St Edmunds, where accounts exist of medieval/post-medieval tunnels in the chalk. In these areas the increasing scale of chalk

quarrying for the cement industry may also have affected the survival of sites, notably around Whitlingham on the bluffs by the River Yare (Fisher 1982) where a skeleton and antler were discovered in old tunnels (Kitton 1878, 436–7). Similarly, housing estates at Durrington in Wiltshire have hidden the land surface and thus removed any opportunity to investigate the presence of further extraction sites here. Overall, the survival of flint mines as earthworks is extremely rare, and as such, threats to their survival from modern land use need serious consideration, particularly at Church Hill, Stoke Down and parts of Harrow Hill, all of which are affected to some extent by the plough.

4
Obtaining the raw material

Utilisation of surface deposits

The extent to which raw material was obtained from surface deposits during prehistory is unclear, but is assumed to have been widespread. Large numbers of sites in the archaeological record are characterised by dense surface scatters of flint debitage with large numbers of cortical flakes, which indicate that local surface material was being exploited. The concentration of such sites at Cranwich in Norfolk, where implements were said to resemble those from Cissbury, is a case in point (Halls 1914, 454–7), as are those at Caister St Edmund where so-called 'Cissbury flint mine type' implements were also recovered (Clarke 1935, 356). These sites all suggest that surface nodules could easily be collected as a result of disturbance to the ground surface, particularly from soil erosion promoted by tree fall, human clearance, or some form of cultivation. In this respect de-forested soils are especially vulnerable to erosion, particularly on slopes such as steep-sided coombs and valleys where flint seams are liable to erode and weathered material gravitates and collects on the lower slopes and valley floors. A number of sites, comprising assemblages with large numbers of cortical flakes, appear in the archaeological record. For example, W31 Wilsford, near Stonehenge (Richards 1990, 164), where a range of 'industrial' debris was recorded; East Horsley in Surrey, where a spread of flint debitage is located on the steep slope of a dry tributary valley of the River Mole (Wood 1952); or Peppard Common, Oxfordshire (Peake 1913; 1914), where a depression containing much debitage was once thought to be a quarry or mine, and debris is again located on the lower slopes of a dry valley. At Grime's Graves too, the exploitation of weathered nodules on the valley floor adjacent to the extant mined area appears to have occurred, and this might have been the stimulus that led to the intensification of extraction.

Extraction from eroding seams

The progression from merely collecting nodules to extracting them from local seams is difficult to demonstrate, but *ad hoc* extraction has been postulated at, for example, the 'factory' at Little Somborne in Hampshire (Clay 1925b, 67) and Maidenhead Thicket in Berkshire (Barnes *et al* 1995). One of the most obvious opportunities for extraction occurs where rivers have cut through chalk formations exposing the flint strata. Perhaps the best-recorded examples lie along the Yare and Wensum Valleys around Norwich where the presence of a number of concentrations of knapping waste indicate the exploitation of surface material eroding from seams along the river bluff. To the west of Norwich, one such site, Ringland, occupies the slopes of the southern bank of the River Wensum (Clarke 1906, 225; 1913, 340–1; 1915a, 148–51). A second at Drayton (NMR number TG 11 SE 12), 4 km to the east, lies on a chalk spur that protrudes from a bluff overlooking the northern bank of the same river. Much struck flint is present at both sites and flint seams lie close to the surface. Indeed, during field investigation at the latter site an exposed seam on one of the steeper slopes was observed where nodules could be extracted with very little effort.

Further potential extraction sites lie adjacent to the flood plain of the River Yare. At Easton, 8 km west of Norwich, a depression in the valley slope was noted in which the presence of knapped flint material was recorded (de Caux 1942), while large numbers of 'Cissbury-like implements' were also recovered from the immediate area (Clarke 1912b, 241). A further site occupies the summit and slopes of a bluff overlooking the river Yare at Algarsthorpe Farm, Great Melton (Clarke and Halls 1917, 374–80). Here an extensive scatter of implements and flakes were recorded covering five fields along some 0.8 km of the riverside. Similar activity occurs at Whitlingham, to the southeast of Norwich. In addition to a series of surface scatters (Healy pers comm), a hoard of flint axes (Halls 1908, 111), and deer antler picks (Norwich County Museum Records), flint flakes and a chipped flint axe have also been recovered from the river itself, and were suggested by the Ordnance Survey to be from 'old flint mines'. Although as yet there is no direct evidence of prehistoric mining, an 18th-century reference to

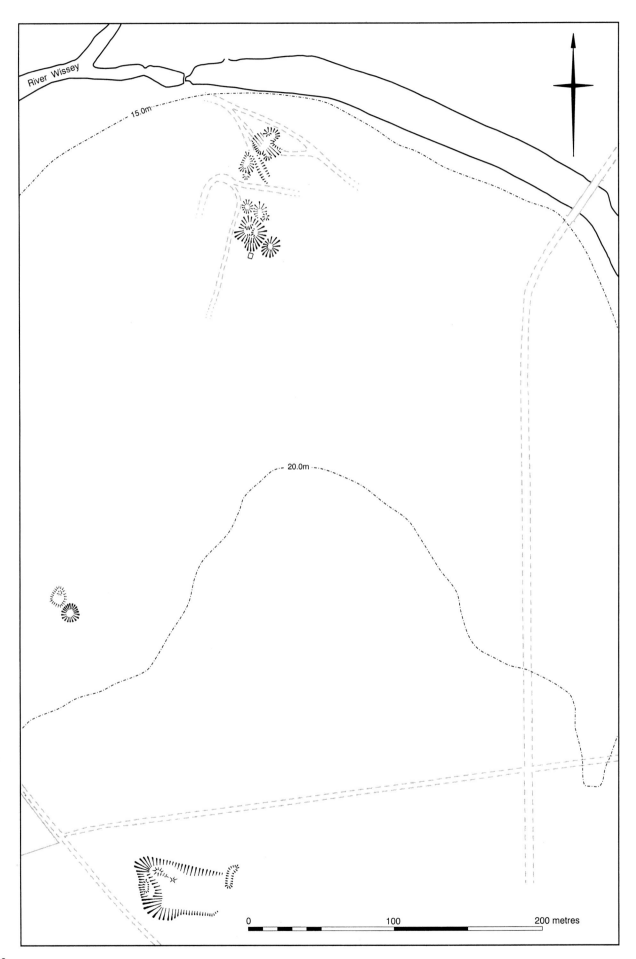

River Wissey

15.0m

20.0m

0   100   200 metres

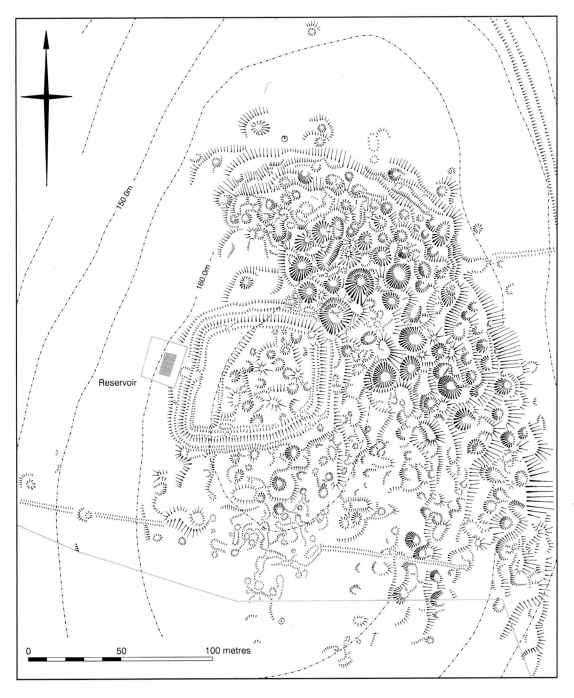

0   50   100 metres

Figure 4.1 (opposite) Earthwork survey of the putative flint mines at Buckenham Toft, Norfolk. The surface has been landscaped and levelled and the shifting sandy soil may also have obscured traces of extraction. The single isolated depression (centre left) is possibly the excavation hollow described by Greenwell (1870, 432) and Clarke (1908, 116). The nature of the series of depressions to the north, close to the river, is unclear.

Figure 4.2 (left) The earthwork survey of Harrow Hill flint mines, West Sussex. Note the superimposition of the later enclosure on the summit of the hill. Construction of the enclosure appears to have occurred during the early 1st millennium BC, over 2,000 years after mining had ceased.

antlers found together with an entire human skeleton in a gallery is intriguing (Kitton 1878, 436–7).

River movement may also have resulted in the erosion of flint seams that in turn led to flint extraction at Buckenham Toft, near Thetford (Figure 4.1). Here quarrying was observed to be stratified below a burnt mound close to the River Wissey (Layard 1922, 491–2, 498), while on a gentle slope nearby a shaft and gallery containing 'many deer's antlers' was recorded (Figure 4.1; Greenwell 1870, 432; Clarke 1908, 116).

Quarrying

While it seems likely that the practice of opencast quarrying of outcropping flint seams was a common practice, only at Harrow Hill (Figures 4.2–4.4) has excavation demonstrated that this took place. Curwen found that opencast quarrying was a precursor to deep extraction (Curwen and Curwen 1926), although earthwork survey during this project suggested that at least some of these surface quarries could be stratigraphically later than the adjacent deep shafts. More recent

Figure 4.3 (above)
Ground-level photograph
of the earthworks at
Harrow Hill.
(AA96/2835)

Figure 4.4 (opposite)
Aerial photograph of the
Harrow Hill flint mines,
showing traces of the
complex extending into
the cultivated field on the
left. (NMR 1006/456)

excavations on the southern edge of the main
mining area confirmed that quarrying took place
there also (Holgate 1991, 39), and it may be that
the linear spoil heaps that follow the contours on
the northern and eastern perimeter of the site
may overlie other quarry workings.

Sieveking (1979) considered that pits cut into
the cryoturbated chalk mud at Grime's Graves represented opencast quarrying. While in both of
these English examples opencast quarrying was
considered almost a prelude to mining by shafts,
elsewhere in Europe, such as the Groot Atelier at
Rijckholt in the Netherlands, massive quarries
were a primary method of extraction (Kraaijenhagen 1981, 7). It remains possible that in England
such large quarries have not been recognised,
although the contiguous linear quarries noted at
certain English mines (see below) may have been
similar in nature.

Pits

From surface evidence alone it is not always clear
whether depressions represent pits or shafts. For
convenience, pits are here arbitrarily distinguished

from shafts as being no more than 3 m in excavated
depth. The six shallow pits discovered fortuitously
at Durrington in Wiltshire, during the excavation
of a pipe trench, were dug initially to extract flint
buried only 0.6 m below the surface, but then
followed the same seam to a greater depth as it
approached the summit of the bluff. Here, at
depths as shallow as 2 m the seam was occasionally
followed by digging a niche at the base of the pit
to allow further nodules to be won (Booth and
Stone 1952); thus at Durrington techniques
responded to changing conditions over comparatively small distances.

This process can also be seen at Martin's
Clump, Hampshire, where seams of flint also lie
relatively close to the surface. Observations taken
during the excavation of a pipe trench in 1984
(Ride 1998) suggest that simple shallow pits,
some little more than 1.5 m in depth, were dug
close to the point of outcrop to provide access to
the seam. The close proximity of large numbers
of small pits to each other (Figure 4.5) with little
evidence for spoil dumps between them supports
the view that relatively shallow mining took place
over large parts of the site. In 1954–5, a single
slightly larger pit was excavated and discovered to

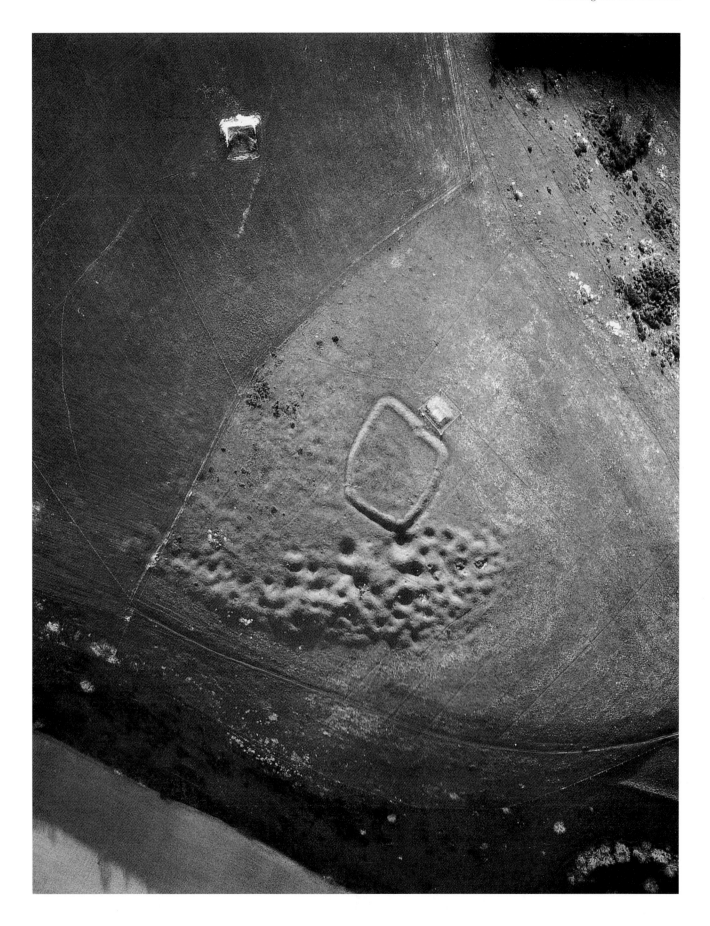

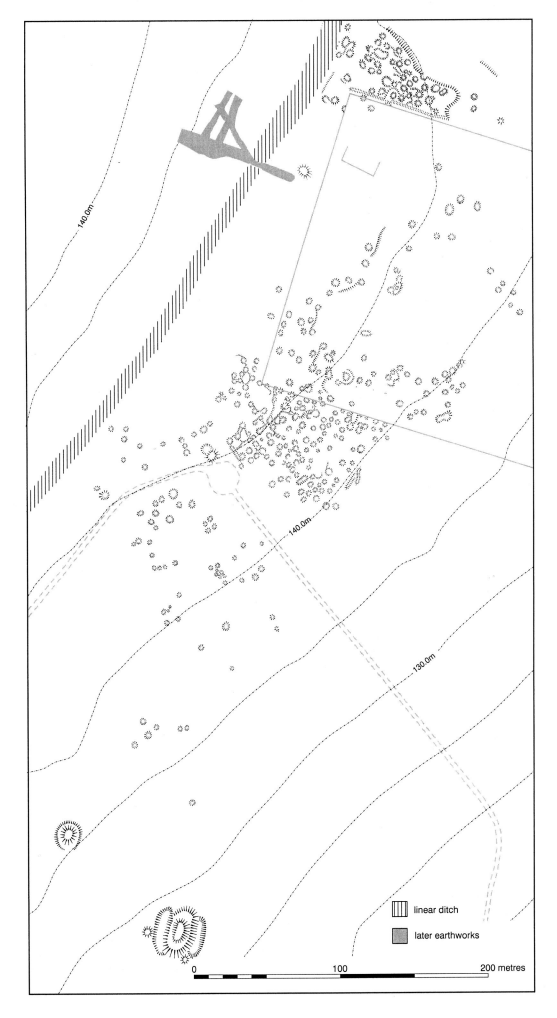

Figure 4.5 The earthwork survey of the flint mines at Martin's Clump, Hampshire. In terms of the number of shafts, this is potentially the largest of the mine complexes. The square enclosure was erected during the course of a failed experiment to re-introduce bustards onto Salisbury Plain during recent times. Subsequently cultivated, the earthworks within have been obscured but are assumed to have once formed a continuous unit with those on either side. To the north, the mines are bounded by a later prehistoric linear ditch. Notice too, the presence of barrows.

Figure 4.6 (opposite) The earthwork survey of the putative flint mines at Tolmere Pond, West Sussex. The more northerly depressions are arranged across the contours and appear not to follow any particular flint seam. Unfortunately, the relationship with the 'Celtic' fields is obscured by later cultivation and a hollow-way that ascends the hillside.

linear ditch

later earthworks

0   100   200 metres

be over 3.0 m in diameter and almost 3.0 m deep (Ride and James 1989; D Ride pers comm) and contained a niche cut into the chalk to extract the maximum flint from the seam.

Armstrong's excavations at Grime's Graves in 1927 discovered that much evidence for mining had been obscured by later cultivation and revealed the presence of simple extraction pits in the valley to the north of the site, which he termed 'primitive pits'. More recently the British Museum also investigated this area and identified a number of small pits, often cutting one another, on the lower slopes of the valley, which were considered to have 'turned over' the whole of that part of the hillside (Sieveking 1979, 13). Armstrong and Sieveking both identified what they described as other forms of extraction, 'intermediate' in scale between these simple pits and the large deep shafts.

At Cissbury, Harrow Hill and Grime's Graves there is a dichotomy between depressions representing small shallow pits and larger excavations thought to be deep shafts. At both Harrow Hill and Grime's Graves there is a distinct geographical distribution to these. At Harrow Hill (Figure 4.2) the smaller pits occur mainly in the south, and across part of the summit but also fill in spaces amongst some of the larger shafts. At Grime's Graves smaller pits can be observed in the north and south, and again they occasionally infill the gaps surrounding some of the larger shafts. There is little direct relationship between the two forms of extraction. Where it does occur there is a suggestion that some smaller pits are later than the shafts (as at Harrow Hill), although they may simply represent an economical method of extracting flint from the relatively shallow seams near the surface. Excavations in the later prehistoric enclosure on the summit of Harrow Hill encountered three pits and part of a fourth (Holleyman 1937). All of these were narrow – two less than c 2.0 m in diameter – and all exploited the same two seams, which lay close together at a depth of between 2.4 m and 3.9 m. The seams were exploited by niches or short galleries at the base of these narrow pits, in a manner similar to those at Durrington and Martin's Clump.

Prospecting pits

The linear series of depressions at Tolmere Pond, Findon, West Sussex, may have been part of the Church Hill complex, and lies roughly across the contours apparently not following a flint seam (Figure 4.6). The separate excavations undertaken here by Curwen and Pull were inconclusive (Curwen and Curwen 1927; Pull archive, Worthing Museum & Art Gallery); neither uncovered

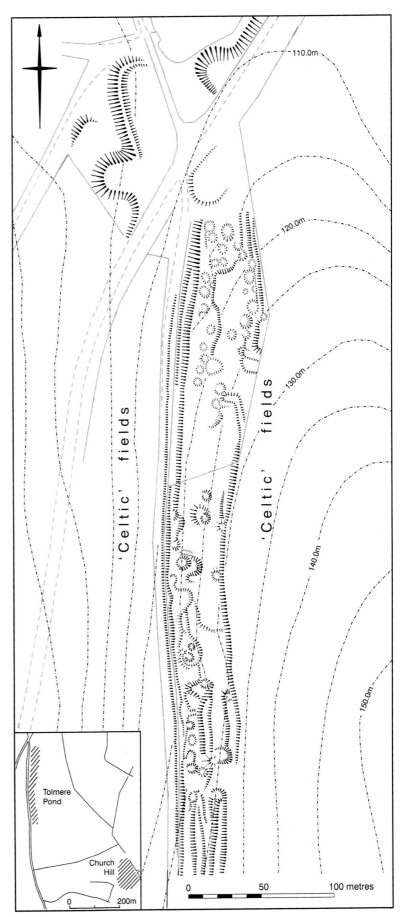

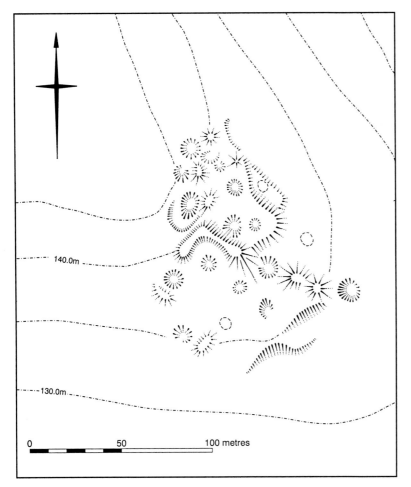

Figure 4.7 The earthwork survey of the flint mines at Church Hill, West Sussex. The site is under cultivation and the once large and deep depressions are now shallow and diffuse.

Figure 4.8 (opposite) Ground-level photograph of the shafts and spoil heaps at Grime's Graves.

evidence of flint extraction, and while the appearance of some depressions closer to the summit might suggest a prehistoric date, the sharp profile of others implies a more recent origin. Given the comparable size of the smaller pits at mines such as Durrington or Martin's Clump, it remains *possible* that some may be Neolithic, which, if so, could represent systematic prospecting across the contours for flint seams.

It is intriguing to note that at Easton Down, of the sample of six shafts excavated by Stone in the 1930s, four did not reach a flint seam. While this proportion is unlikely to have occurred over the site as a whole, that such a high percentage of potentially abortive shafts should occur at all might be considered unusual, given the coomb-head location and the fact that the outcropping seam must have been relatively straightforward to follow along the contour. In comparison to the two larger more successful shafts, these were all relatively narrow – in one case only 1.25 m wide – space enough for only one miner. If these were indeed mine shafts they may have been for prospecting, but arguably other less obvious uses may have underpinned the digging of these pits (*see* Chapter 5).

Similar narrow cylindrical shafts excavated on the lower valley slopes at Grime's Graves were considered by Sieveking (1979) to have been dug to test for the flint seam at a known depth. Like those at Easton Down, some were little over 1 m in diameter, and although sunk through cryoturbated chalk mud and solid chalk to a depth of 6–7 m, they were equally unsuccessful in locating 'floorstone'.

Shafts

Shafts are arbitrarily distinguished from pits by having a depth of over 3 m. In general they provided access to multiple flint seams, and a platform (the base of the shaft) from which sprang underground adits or galleries. Most shafts are of comparatively large diameter, generally between 10 m and 15 m, which contrasts with those of the gunflint miners which were significantly narrower. The large dimensions of the Neolithic shafts are usually explained in terms of a large workforce. Felder (1981, 57–62) has quantified this and using these principles Sieveking (1979) suggested that the larger mine shafts at Grime's Graves represent organised exploitation compared to the small pits on the valley floor which might be associated with extraction by individuals.

The proximity of shafts to each other is of interest. Closely packed pits exploiting shallow seams near the surface is an obvious strategy to maximise the extraction of flint. However, the same does not apply to deeper shafts where lower seams can be more efficiently exploited by underground galleries. One shaft at Church Hill (Pull's no. 6; *see* Figures 2.8 and 4.7) was so close to its neighbour (Pull's no. 7), that there was little more than 0.5 m of chalk between them, and Pull noted that they occupied the same surface depression (Pull 1953, 18; Pull archive, Worthing Museum & Art Gallery). The apparent pairing of shafts enclosed by a common spoil heap is a common feature at Grime's Graves (Figure 4.8) where some shafts appear to be differentially backfilled, one frequently being deeper than its neighbour, suggesting different depositional histories. This can be illustrated by the observations of Peake (1915, 93) who recorded the different directions and frequency with which chalk had been dumped into Pits 1 and 2 at Grime's Graves, and who concluded that several adjacent shafts had been open simultaneously. Felder (1981, 60), in comparing the flint mines at Rijckholt in the Netherlands with those at Grime's Graves, suggested that in the deeper shafts safety considerations were a greater consideration, and that an escape route would have been needed. At Rijckholt it was suggested

that paired shafts were dug simultaneously and then connected underground which would allow one shaft to be exploited while a second remained open for emergencies. Alternatively, such an arrangement may have been for practical convenience, perhaps to allow the sharing of lifting tackle. Although the degree to which paired shafts were worked simultaneously is unknown, the available evidence suggests that at Grime's Graves at least, it was not unusual to have more than one shaft open at any one time.

Complex sites: extraction of multiple seams

Certain mines appear to have been sunk to extract as much raw material as possible from the strata, despite the varying quality of flint from the different seams. It is clear that at most Sussex mines more than one seam was exploited, shafts being sunk to different levels on the hillslope, but this is probably best demonstrated at Harrow Hill which has witnessed a number of well-recorded excavations this century. The Curwens' excavations in 1925 encountered three seams of flint, and Felder's in 1982 four (McNabb *et al* 1996), all of which inclined obliquely against the slope of the hillside. If mining had progressed uphill the shafts would rapidly have become very deep if they followed the same seam, and other seams higher in the profile would have been encountered, which themselves could be open quarried at the point of outcrop, and thereafter by deeper shafts (Figure 4.9). Curwen noted that an upper seam outcropped where his excavated shaft, Pit 21, had been dug; the shaft thus potentially destroying any evidence of opencast workings,

Figure 4.9 A hypothetical extraction sequence. First, surface quarrying exploits outcropping flint, which is then followed upslope by increasingly deeper shafts. Note that gradually the lower workings become buried beneath the spoil dumps from the later shafts.

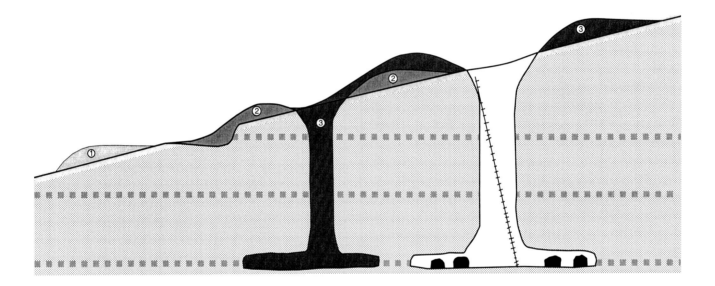

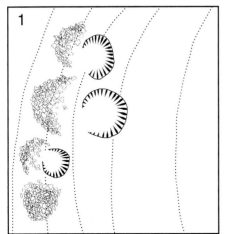

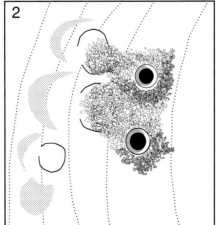

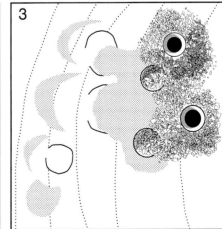

but a recess in the wall of the shaft suggested that the upper seam had in fact been worked. A further seam outcropped some 30 m to the north of the excavated shaft, and Curwen discovered other evidence for opencast activity where it lay close to the surface. Within the excavated shaft, galleries did not follow this seam very far, as it was an easy task to sink another pit to this level alongside the main shaft. Such surface quarrying was often obscured by spoil dumps from later deeper excavations. Evidence for a similarly complex extraction process was discovered at Church Hill; four flint seams were recorded in Shaft 4 (Pull 1953); raw material from the third seam had been extracted by niches, while galleries were used to extract flint from the fourth and lowest seam.

In contrast, the deep shafts that have been excavated at Grime's Graves have provided no clear evidence that the higher seams of 'wallstone' were extracted, although Sieveking pointed out that shallow recesses in the shaft wall of Greenwell's Pit might indicate that it was. However, it may be that some of the shallow depressions adjacent to the larger shafts were designed to extract the 'wallstone' between the larger pits, as at Harrow Hill. Extraction on several levels was certainly taking place on the valley floor, two-level pits being recorded which exploited both chalk mud and the underlying chalk for flint (Sieveking 1979, and *see* below), while in Pit 8 (Longworth and Varndell 1996) attempts were made to reach a seam at a lower level by sinking a trial hole from the floor of the pit.

Complex sites: linear quarries

Although strictly undated, the small site on Nore Down may represent a further method of extracting flint from more than one seam (Figure 4.10). Here, two parallel ditch-like features that cut progressively deeper into the hillside were originally thought to be the flanking ditches of a long barrow (Aldsworth 1979). However, excavation within one of the 'ditches' revealed a feature which appeared to be the upper part of a shaft (Aldsworth 1983). Similar linear hollows can be observed cutting into the hillside at Long Down (Figure 4.11). Salisbury (1961) partially excavated within one of these and also encountered a feature described as a shaft, similar to that excavated at Nore Down, but this time with an unusual rectangular plan, and which produced axe roughouts and broken antler. Although only partly confirmed by excavation, this technique appears to represent initial large-scale open-pit quarrying of a seam, followed by the sinking of shafts to a lower seam

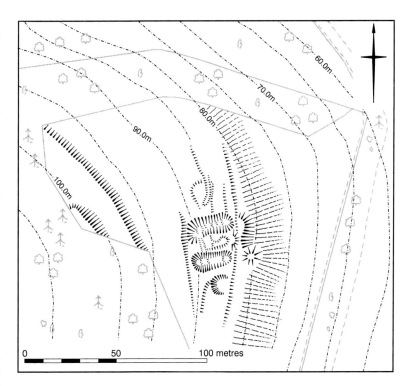

from the quarry floor. Surface evidence suggests that this technique was used at other sites also, in particular at Grime's Graves (Figure 4.12) where in some cases it involves pairs of conjoined shafts, but in others extends dramatically in a linear fashion or occasionally in small clusters. In these cases the surface has been quarried to a depth of between 1 and 3 m with depressions marking the position of shafts to deeper levels in the base of the quarries. Such linear and clustered open-pit quarries at Grime's Graves incorporate up to eleven shafts within them.

Development of earthworks

The fluid nature of spoil dumps and their sporadic depositional histories pose some restrictions on the interpretation of site chronology from surface evidence alone. The form of the spoil dumps cannot provide typological information to construct sequences. In terms of the physical remains of the mines, the most striking difference lies between the prehistoric examples and the post-medieval gunflint pits at Brandon (*see* Figure 3.1), particularly the spacing between shafts, the scale of the shafts, and differences in the form of the waste dumps. At Brandon this was attributable to the impact of social conventions or mining law (Skertchley 1879) and the organisation of the industry. This helped to ensure that safe boundaries were kept between pits and that virgin areas were worked systematically.

Figure 4.10 The earthwork survey of the putative flint mines at Nore Down, West Sussex. The open-pit quarries cut into the hillside, from which shafts were probably sunk to seams at a lower level.

*Figure 4.11 The
earthwork survey of the
flint mines at Long
Down, West Sussex.
Even though several
sequences of cultivation
can be recognised the
mines still form a
compact unit. Notice
how the shafts are
arranged in tiers along
the contours, with waste
material dumped
downhill from each shaft.
Note also how the linear
open-pit quarries cut into
the hillside. Excavations
within one of these
encountered the top of a
shaft, which may have
been sunk to extract flint
from a lower seam.*

*Figure 4.12 (opposite)
Earthwork survey of the
flint mines at Grime's
Graves, Norfolk. Note in
particular how the larger,
deeper shafts, shown by
heavier hachuring,
concentrate in the east.
The dual shafts, and
linear open-pit quarries
are clearly visible.*

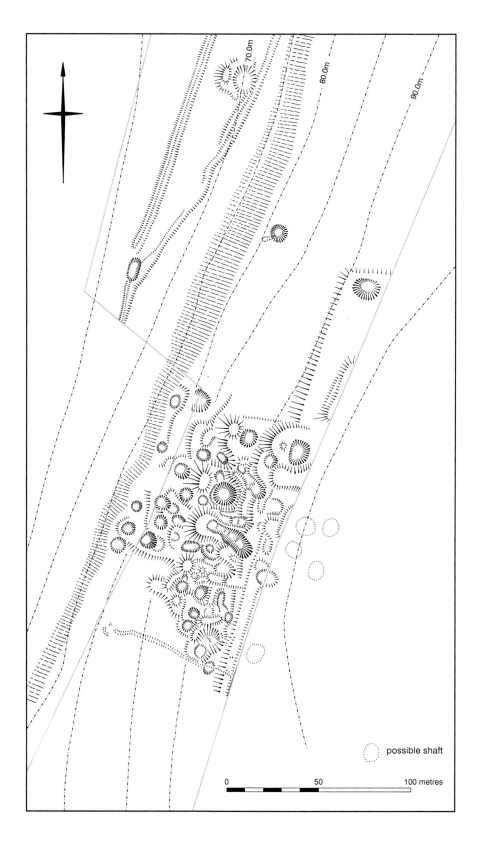

70.0m

80.0m

90.0m

possible shaft

0   50   100 metres

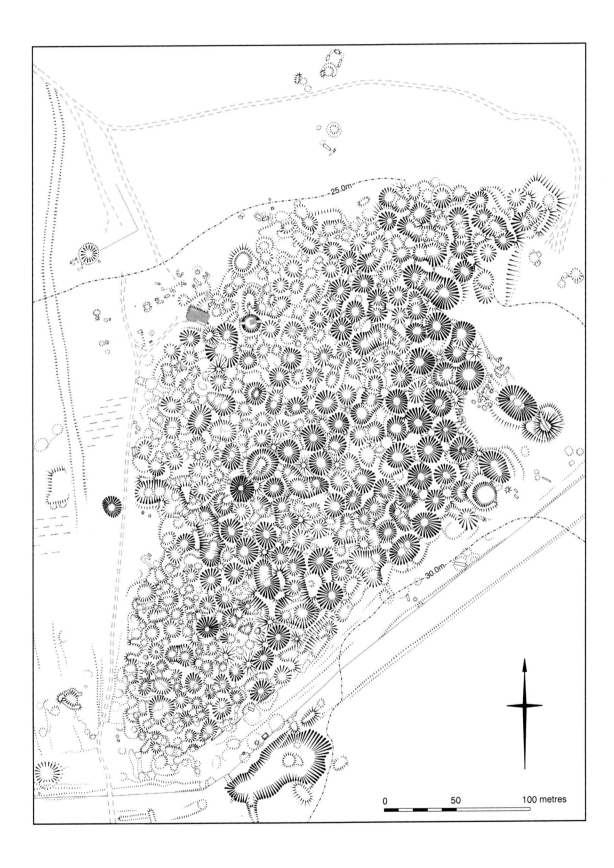

0   50   100 metres

Extraction pits and shafts

At Long Down (Figure 4.11) the surface remains of extraction pits and deeper shafts are still visible as depressions on the slope of the hillside. Their surface morphology varies from sub-circular to rectilinear in plan, in part reflecting the subsequent development of weathering cones, the post-deposition of spoil from later shafts, the erosion of nearby spoil heaps into shafts, and in some cases later ploughing. Differences also exist between the larger, deeper depressions and the small shallow examples, which could reflect differing amounts of backfilling but may alternatively indicate that seams of differing depths were being exploited.

At Grime's Graves the pits and shafts vary considerably in size, both in diameter and depth, and are normally located close together, separated by little more than a few metres (Figures 3.4 and 4.12). In general, the smaller, shallower shafts are placed around the northern and western slopes, and in the south-west corner of the site. In contrast, the larger and deeper shafts, although not confined exclusively to the higher ground, tend to cluster in the south and east. The range of sizes is enormous, the largest – a slightly oval depression – is 22.0 m by 20.0 m with a depth of 2.3 m; the deepest depression being slightly over 3 m.

Whether the 'circular' form of shaft was significant is unclear. On the surface many shafts appear to be oval or sub-rectangular, although differential weathering may have affected the final shape of many depressions. The shaft of the 'Cave Pit' at Cissbury was found to be rectangular in shape (Park-Harrison 1877b), as was the example revealed at Long Down (Salisbury 1961). While the circular plan form may have been more efficient to excavate, the presence of squared corners in some shafts may have been of some practical use, perhaps for securing ladders or providing support for platforms. A buttress was recorded in the 'Cave Pit' at Cissbury that may have provided a similar facility.

The surface remains of the spoil dumps make it difficult to identify access routes from any particular direction, most dumps appearing as unbroken encircling rings of waste. One of the larger shafts at Cissbury appears to have an entrance break on the downhill side. However, at Lingheath Farm, Brandon, the recent gunflint miners, unlike their Neolithic predecessors, had a different method of waste dumping. In general they placed their spoil on either side of the shaft leaving one or two access points, thus creating horse-shoe or 'hengiform' shaped dumps to allow areas to place nodules lifted from the shafts (*see* Figure 3.1).

The extraction sequence

In Sussex the dramatic topography of the South Downs appears to have influenced directly the process of extraction. In general, shafts were initially placed along the false crest of a ridge, often at the interface of chalk and Clay-with-flints. Unfortunately, the damage at Blackpatch has obscured much of this information; however, from the evidence of shaft distribution it seems possible that the flint seam outcropped on the false crest, and was worked from a westerly direction (Figure 4.13). Similarly, at Church Hill, any detailed sequence of extraction is difficult to establish, but here too, it seems likely that mining started on the steep slopes in the east where the flint seam may have outcropped, and subsequently mining worked upslope towards the summit. If extraction at this site began by quarrying an exposed outcrop, it is likely that the hangar to the east (not shown on Figure 4.7), just within the grounds of Findon Place Park, may be of some importance. Field reconnaissance noted many struck flakes exposed in treeholes in this area. A similar sequence appears to be demonstrated at Long Down and Cissbury. At the latter site the surface evidence suggests that mining started on the north-western side of the hill where the slope is extremely steep and where erosion is likely to have exposed the flint seam.

Sites comprising randomly scattered pits or shafts

The earthwork survey of Easton Down (Figure 4.14) demonstrates that shafts were dug at very different heights on the floor, sides and around the edge of a coomb in no apparent order. They do not appear to follow any one seam of raw material and the unusual irregular spacing might imply that the site developed sporadically. Field investigation suggests that a number of seams outcrop in the area, although these are rarely mentioned or illustrated in Stone's excavation accounts (Stone 1931a; 1931b; 1933a; 1933b; 1935). The position of the shafts suggests that there appears to have been no single favoured seam.

Tiers of shafts

Certain mines such as Long Down, Cissbury, Harrow Hill and possibly Church Hill and Blackpatch, indicate a slightly more organised approach. Here there is no surface evidence of the position of the flint seam, but in each case steep downland slopes imply that erosion might have exposed a flint seam. At Long Down it is likely that the earliest activity lies beneath the lower of the scarps (partly overlain by later lynchets in the north-west) that bound the western side of the site (*see* Figure 4.11): this observation would explain the knapping debris found extensively in this area. Assuming the seam(s) at Long Down were reasonably horizontal, this would have necessitated the excavation of gradually deeper shafts as mining moved upslope. The shafts, which are loosely arranged in tiered rows ranged along the contours, provide some evidence for a chronological sequence from the juxtaposition of overlapping spoil heaps downslope which suggests that extraction moved uphill (the slightly confusing

palimpsest on the upper, easternmost, edge of the earthworks has resulted from the incomplete destruction of the spoil dumps by the later ploughing, giving the misleading impression that the earlier dumps actually overlie the later lynchet).

In a similar fashion, the shafts lying above the steep north-western slope at Cissbury appear to be arranged in tiers along the contours, those downslope probably representing earlier mines in the

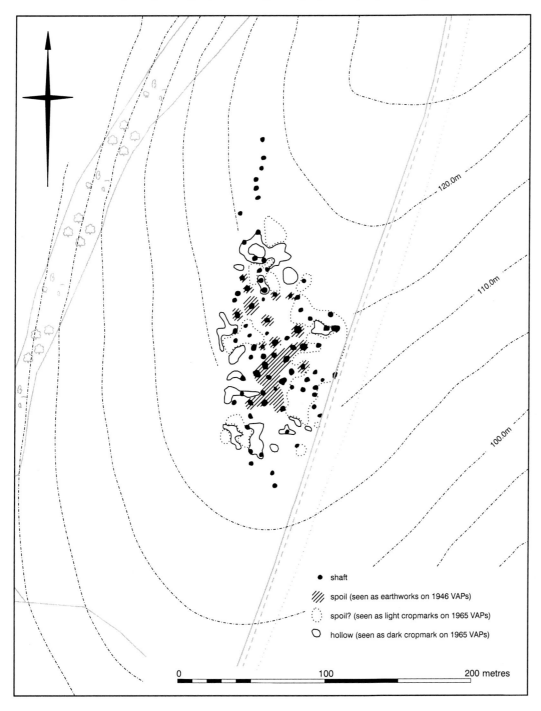

- shaft
- spoil (seen as earthworks on 1946 VAPs)
- spoil? (seen as light cropmarks on 1965 VAPs)
- hollow (seen as dark cropmark on 1965 VAPs)

0   100   200 metres

Figure 4.13 Aerial transcription of the flint mines at Blackpatch, West Sussex. The surface remains were bulldozed in the early 1950s, but ground survey demonstrates some slight earthwork evidence still survives.

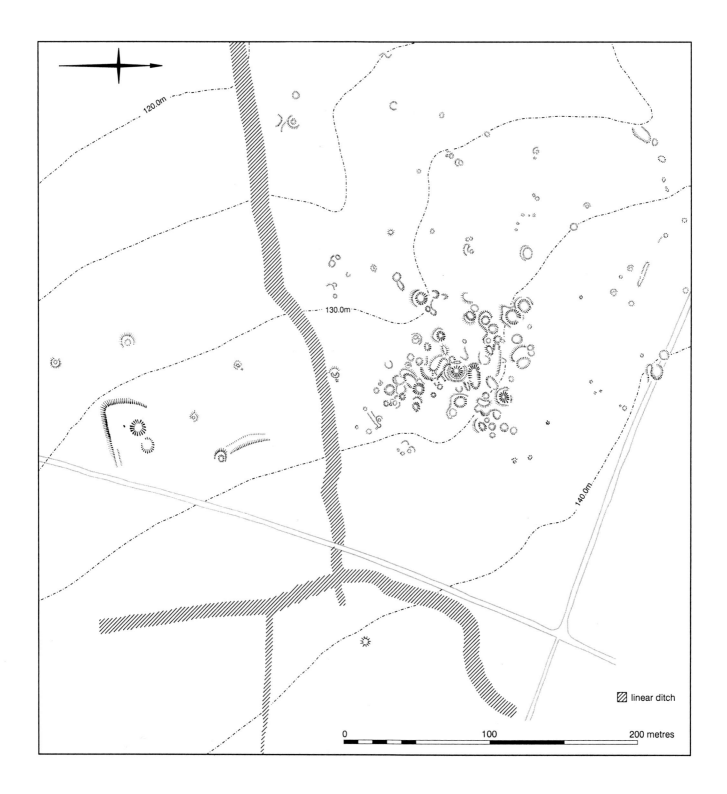

legend: linear ditch

0   100   200 metres

120.0m
130.0m
140.0m

sequence; the tier situated upon the false crest incorporates some of the largest shafts in Sussex, with some depressions exceeding 20 m in diameter. These shafts lying on the false crest were late in the development of the mine, their large size suggesting a more labour-intensive approach.

Methods of waste management

At Long Down, and other Sussex sites on sloping terrain such as Cissbury, Harrow Hill, Church Hill and Blackpatch, the shafts and pits are surrounded by spoil dumps forming mounds or linear banks surviving up to 2 m in height, but like the shafts with weathered or plough-damaged profiles, some spoil has invariably spilled into the shafts obscuring the division between the upper lip of the shaft and spoil heap. The usual method of extraction appears to have been to place the spoil downslope to avoid spillage back into the shaft. In so doing this may have buried a number of earlier disused shafts beneath the later spoil heaps. This might also explain how some shafts were partially backfilled during the course of excavating new shafts, rather than as a deliberate policy of backfilling.

At Church Hill a two-fold approach to waste disposal appears to have been used with dumps pushed downhill from the tiered shafts in the east and south, but on more level areas the waste was placed centrally between groups of shafts. In the centre of the mined area an unusual angular spoil heap remains a prominent feature and probably overlies other buried shafts.

Linear spoil heaps are also found at Harrow Hill where they may indicate some of the earliest activity on site – the areas of primary quarrying at the outcropping flint seam. At Cissbury, earlier dumps of mining debris may have been incorporated into the rampart of the later fort which has many irregularities adjacent to the mines, its course perhaps determined by the existence of linear spoil heaps. Such dumps are located downslope from the shafts, particularly those lying upon the false crest; some are quite massive and often form linear arrangements that link shafts along the contours. Unfortunately, the hillfort ditch obscures some detail, but spoil can be seen protruding from beneath the counterscarp bank in places.

At Grime's Graves spoil heaps are closely set around the lip of each shaft and vary dramatically from relatively low examples of 0.5 m or 1.0 m to massive dumps over 2.0 m high, and are invariably mounded at the junctions of three or more shafts (Figure 4.8). Spoil mounded at these intersections has invariably eroded into all shafts including, presumably, the shaft from which it originated. Only very rarely on those more level areas does the spoil from one shaft demonstrably

overlap another so that it is possible to determine a sequence. Consequently, the study of spoil heap stratigraphy can only partly illustrate the chronological development across a site. Where such sequences have been recorded at Grime's Graves it would appear that mining generally progressed in a southerly direction. Occasionally, linear spoil dumps were placed alongside two or more shafts, effectively linking them, but there is no discernable pattern to this, and it would appear that spoil was simply deposited in the most convenient places. Overall, there seems to have been little effort to keep the area around each new shaft clear of spoil or to ensure that accessways around old shafts were maintained. The deliberate mounding of spoil between shafts is curious, given that it would be easier to simply tip waste into adjacent abandoned shafts. Indeed, while subterranean waste management must have played a part, spoil dumps do cover a considerable area of the ground surface and must also have gradually buried many earlier shafts and other ancillary features.

Patterns among the earthworks

The corpus of new surveys suggests that in addition to *ad hoc* quarrying at outcrops, at least six other methods of exploiting the flint seams were used:

TECHNIQUE	SITE
1 Small circular or sub-circular pits:	Easton Down, Martin's Clump, Blackpatch, Church Hill, Grime's Graves; the southern spur at Cissbury; the southern summit at Harrow Hill;
2 Small paired pits, linked by a common spoil heap:	Grime's Graves;
3 Large single shafts:	Blackpatch, Church Hill, Grime's Graves, Cissbury, Harrow Hill, Long Down;
4 Large paired shafts, linked by a common spoil heap:	Cissbury and Grime's Graves;
5 Open quarries, paired two stage working:	Grime's Graves;
6 Open quarries, linear or grouped, two stage working:	Linear at Nore Down, Long Down and Grime's Graves; trefoil or quatrefoil in shape at Grime's Graves.

Figure 4.14 (opposite) The earthwork survey of the flint mines at Easton Down, Wiltshire. The extant remains are situated around the head of a narrow coomb. On the basis of the presence of knapping debris, Stone (1931a) considered the mined area to be much more extensive, and to the south of the existing shafts lies an area covered by traces of 'Celtic' fields which may mask further extraction. He also recorded spreads of Beaker pottery, and a number of excavated pits and other features that he described as representing Beaker settlement. Notice too, the presence of a round barrow to the south and long flint cairn to the north of the mines, the latter excavated by Stone to reveal a series of Collared Urns and cremation deposits. The linear ditch is of later prehistoric date.

Notwithstanding a chronological gap rated in hundreds of years, techniques employed in the Sussex sites that developed in response to the local topography appear to have been adopted, or rediscovered, in East Anglia. Here, on more gentle terrain, the whole range of extraction techniques was employed (Figure 4.15), the plan of Grime's Graves (Figure 4.12) revealing examples of possible two-level working amongst the surviving earthworks. The deep dual and linear open quarries containing shallow depressions ranged along their floors all appear to have been dug to the base of the overlying sand/boulder clay layer. In the case of the sand this may have been relatively easy to remove, although its stability would have caused problems and perhaps led to the use of revetting around the mouths of the shafts. Such a process would lay bare the uppermost 'topstone' layer of flint, and is in essence a form of 'open-pit' quarrying which provided a convenient base from which to sink shafts to the 'floorstone' further below. Even though it was part of a two-stage mining process such features are here termed quarries in order to differentiate them from mine shafts which appear to have developed as a single episode.

The linear open-pit quarries are sometimes complex. One example situated upon the western edge of Grime's Graves is roughly 1 m deep and extends for some 80 m in length, incorporating at least ten shallow depressions left by the presence of former shafts ranged along its base. The quarry begins on the edge of the surviving minefield and follows an erratic course to the south respecting shafts to the north and east. However, it is noticeable that the quarry does not lie along the contours, and it may be that it fossilises a general trend of extracting the seam towards the south-west. A further, but smaller example of this extraction technique lies in the southern part of the complex, incorporating at least six shafts. This quarry changes direction and doubles back on itself before belling out into a trefoil-like arrangement at its southern end. Interestingly there is a large irregular spoil dump in the centre of this meandering quarry, perhaps implying a common approach to waste management. It is difficult to be certain which shaft began this sequence, but the group appears to avoid two earlier shafts lying immediately to the north. Quarried to a depth of up to 2.7 m, the shafts appear as slight depressions on the quarry floor, and again much of the chalk surface thus exposed would have provided space for activities around the head of the shaft.

The groups of linear quarries and conjoined shafts provide some of the best evidence for site development. Paired shafts, linear and grouped quarries are all likely to represent discrete episodes of activity, arguably over short timescales. Most of the well-preserved paired shafts at Grime's Graves follow the contours suggesting that flint was being extracted first from the shallowest areas. In contrast, other pairings situated within the same areas cut across the contours, suggesting that mining was *ad hoc* and not systematic. The linear quarries provide similar evidence and indicate the former presence of sizeable, unexploited areas. While those on the north-eastern edge arguably follow the contours, one example in the west lies across the slope, while others change direction as though they were avoiding pre-existing shafts. Several large single pits lie between linear quarry groups, some of which may have preceded quarries, and might represent a less intensive and more episodic phase of extraction. Elsewhere the presence of smaller shafts may represent the exploitation of gaps left between the main areas of extraction.

In the south-western part of Grime's Graves, small individual pits or shafts appear to have been the prevailing method of extraction, although they are often clustered around larger pits. This situation also occurs in the north-east where much of the small-scale mining appears to be infilling around slightly larger shafts. Armstrong's (1927) view was that there was a chronological and evolutionary development from small to large extraction pits, whereas Peake (1915, 93) had previously suggested that the cluster of small shafts in the south-west corner might be of a relatively later date. These contrary viewpoints were addressed by work by the British Museum (Sieveking *et al* 1973, 201; Sieveking 1979, fig 15) which has produced a series of radiocarbon dates indicating that some of the small shafts and pits may in fact be later than the large examples, thus emphasising the limits of site morphology as a chronological tool. Contrary to Armstrong's view of continuous evolutionary development from the 'primitive pits' in the valley to the large shafts in the area of Greenwell's Pit, the combined results of this survey and the British Museum project suggest that the site developed sporadically rather than in a systematic manner.

Subterranean workings

With the possible exception of the randomly scattered pits at Easton Down, the surface evidence at most mines indicates that there was an attempt to extract the maximum amounts of flint. In this respect the densely packed surface plans must reflect equally busy activity below ground. Excluding the preliminary investigation of thirty shafts at Cissbury by Lane Fox, and the partially excavated examples at Nore Down and Long Down, over forty-three shafts and 120 workfloors have been excavated at various Neolithic flint mines. While

Figure 4.15 (opposite) Terrain model (a) shown alongside an interpretative diagram (b) of Grime's Graves.

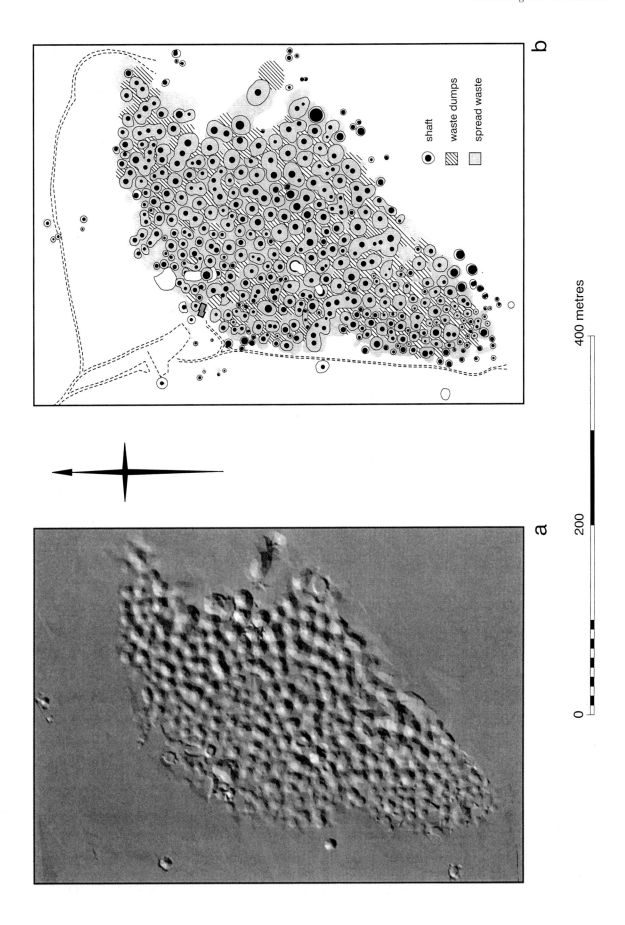

some early reports underplayed the role of galleries as providing simply a means of supplementing the flint obtained from the floors of the shafts, the primary aim would appear to have been to extract the maximum raw material following the investment of labour in having dug the shaft. Much flint was certainly extracted from the shaft floor, but in the deeper mines the shaft was primarily a means of access to the wider seam. The complexity achieved by some galleries is illustrated in Lane Fox's (1876) plan of some of the Cissbury galleries (Figure 2.4), and later by Pull's plan of galleries on the south spur at Cissbury and more recently – and perhaps the only genuinely accurate plans we have – by Felder at Harrow Hill (Figure 4.16) and Grime's Graves (Longworth and Varndell 1996, fig 4; McNabb et al 1996, 25). These

excavations have shown that galleries frequently interconnect with those of adjacent shafts, but in many cases this was coincidental rather than a deliberate intention. Plans of the subterranean workings (Figure 4.16) show that invariably the whole floor area is mined away, leaving only a thin wall or pillars of chalk to support the roof, a technique now referred to as pillar mining in European literature (Borkowski 1995a, 73).

The development of further subterranean techniques does not appear to have occurred: no extensive chambers have been encountered in Britain to match those of Poland (Borkowski 1995a, 73–4) or Italy (Di Lernia et al 1995). However, only a small percentage of shafts have been excavated. Thus it is possible that such workings may exist in England. In this context it might be

possible that the hard cement-like chalk of York-shire would have been particularly suitable for this form of extraction if mining took place in this region.

Unlike the 19th-century gunflint mines where systematic methods of extraction were observed and described in detail (Figure 3.3; Skertchley 1879), no uniform pattern can be identified among the Neolithic galleries. Underground restrictions may have created problems and inhib-ited the levels of accuracy in some early plans – in many reports there is a complete absence of plans – all making interpretation difficult. However, it may be that some of the straighter galleries, such as those at Cissbury recorded by Lane Fox (Figure 2.4), were designed to allow the rope haulage of large nodules from the seam to the shaft (Felder

pers comm), whereas the short curving examples at Church Hill and Blackpatch illustrated by Pull (Figure 4.16) may reflect a more *ad hoc* approach.

Workshop processing

Many of the heaps, mounds and depressions around the shafts have been created by the care-fully managed dumping of waste. However, some must also represent working areas and concentra-tions of manufacturing debris. Such features are poorly understood because most excavation has tended to focus upon the shafts. At some sites a number of small shallow depressions up to 12 metres wide have been recorded, which lie among the spoil heaps and are structurally unlike

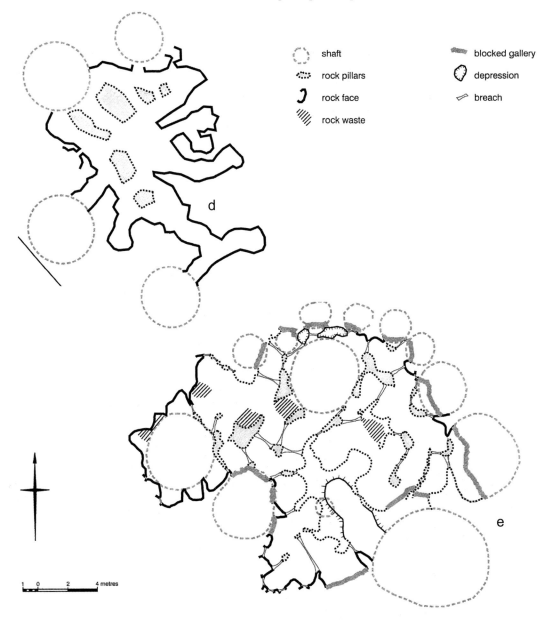

shaft
rock pillars
rock face
rock waste
blocked gallery
depression
breach

1   0   2   4 metres

backfilled shafts. At Long Down examples occur upon the summits of the waste dumps, or in three cases are found adjacent to the lips of shafts or at the base of spoil heaps. At Harrow Hill certain of the larger shafts appear to be associated with two such platforms.

At Grime's Graves over twenty similar shallow hollows or level areas have been tentatively interpreted as working platforms. They are placed immediately adjacent to the mouths of the shafts and are surrounded by spoil, suggesting that they were not part of the waste management system. Although interpretation is problematic, their location and form suggest that they represent working areas or the position where mining apparatus stood.

Many workfloors originally found within the mine complexes are likely to have been destroyed and the material redistributed by later phases of activity. Despite this, the excavation of knapping floors has demonstrated that much primary dressing of nodules was carried out immediately adjacent to the mines. At Cissbury, an area adjacent to one shaft, recorded after scrub clearance, consisted of a concentration of struck flint flakes of various sizes ranging from large cores to minute spalls. This 'in situ' deposit provides evidence that certain artefacts were at least roughed out on site, although whether contemporary with the adjacent shaft is not clear. Flint waste was also recovered by Lane Fox at Cissbury from beneath the rectangular enclosure 100 m to the north-east of the mines (see Figure 3.6), while excavations of a lynchet in the south-eastern part of the hillfort (Curwen and Ross-Williamson 1931) also recovered evidence of knapping. At Church Hill, Pull recorded workshop debris on the hillslope 50–70 m to the south of the mine complex. Similarly the results of fieldwalking at Grime's Graves suggests that initial knapping was carried out quite close to the point of extraction, illustrated by a rapid fall-off in the density of struck flint some 200 m from the shafts.

Organisation

The evidence of the mines, particularly the deep shafts, implies a level of social organisation and technological specialisation far beyond an *ad hoc* level of exploitation. This may be illustrated by the sheer scale of some of the shafts which have been interpreted as potentially allowing twenty people to work in them simultaneously (Felder 1981). Shafts are invariably found packed closely together, presumably to maximise the extraction potential, which combined with the radiating galleries all suggests a well-organised extraction strategy for individual shafts.

The flint mine sites of Sussex, together with other Neolithic monuments on the chalk, have been used to model territorial boundaries and attempt to recreate local social landscapes based upon each community having its respective causewayed enclosure, long barrows and flint mine (Drewett 1978, 27). This assumes that mines formed part of a local territorial arrangement and that they were not worked by visitors from a wide area. There is little evidence on this count, however the local groups were structured, they must have had a sound knowledge of the provenance of flint outcrops and the requisite skills to exploit them. The chance finds of ground axes around Harrow Hill and Cissbury concentrate on the coastal plain, rather than around the mines, and suggest that settlement activity may be centred on the lower ground. The exploitation of flint may have been a component of the local Neolithic economy, whether based upon pastoralism or sedentary practices, and might even have been a seasonal activity. Furthermore, assuming the demand for raw material was similar in all areas, the restricted distribution of flint mines implies that the Sussex, Wessex and Breckland sites must have supplied material to much of England, although the details of this at a regional or national level are difficult to define at present.

5
The role of flint mines in Neolithic society

The mines in their landscape setting

As the previous chapter makes clear, the choice of locations for flint mining was inevitably constrained by the presence or otherwise of suitable flint, the availability of which may have been advertised by the outcropping or erosion of seams. Interestingly, many mines do not appear to slavishly follow the course of the flint strata. Likewise, it is not always the best quality or the most accessible flint sources that were exploited by mining. It may be the case, therefore, that the location already possessed some significance which led to it being favoured for flint mining, rather than the best quality raw material in the area being sought out. The landscape is already likely to have been deeply imbued with ritual and social significance before the beginning of the Neolithic (Tilley 1994). Particular locations may have become important because of their place in the seasonal or cyclical range of activities, either in terms of resources (food, raw materials, shelter) or as places where different groups periodically gathered. Other places may have acquired significance simply through their presence as prominent features in the physical landscape, or through a combination of such factors. Prominent, dramatic and awe-inspiring locations such as the axe 'factories' at Penmaenmawr, Tievebulliagh, or Great Langdale are obvious points of reference here, as they are both highly conspicuous landscape features and stone resources which were exploited during the Neolithic. However, as recent work at Langdale (Bradley and Edmonds 1993) has highlighted, ease of access and quality of the raw material do not necessarily determine the location of the preferred quarry sites.

The careful placing of sites within the landscape was a widespread phenomenon that can be recognised throughout the Neolithic and Bronze Age (Barrett et al 1991; Bradley 1993). The long barrows of the English chalklands exhibit a distinct preference for locations close to springs, streams or rivers. Others may have been deliberately placed close to flint mines (Martin's Clump, Easton Down), causewayed enclosures (eg Robin Hood's Ball, Hambledon Hill), or cursus monuments such as Dorchester, Oxon (Atkinson et al 1951; Bradley and Chambers 1988), and Dorset (Barrett et al 1991, 36–43). Causewayed enclosures in particular occupy locations which can mirror those of certain sites in the preceding Mesolithic, the most frequent location being prominent gravel knolls overlooking lowland rivers. This may continue a tradition of established meeting places or camp sites. However, other causewayed enclosures occur on downland scarps or summits, their heightened visibility from one or more directions appearing to be an equally important consideration.

The environmental setting of the flint mines

Environmental data for the English flint mines is limited in both quantity and quality, but what there is points to the mines originally being established in woodland settings (Ellis 1986). Among the South Downs group, only Harrow Hill (Curwen and Curwen 1926, 126–9; Holleyman 1937, 246–8), Blackpatch (Goodman et al 1924; Pull 1932) and Long Down (Salisbury 1961) have seen recovery of environmental evidence, though the processes of collection obviously fall far short of what would be expected today (see Thomas 1982). Recovery of mollusca seems to have been largely by hand, and will have focused on the shaft fills. Thus some of the fauna at least will relate to the damp and shaded conditions likely to be prevalent in such places. Although a detailed chronological sequence is impossible to recreate at present, it would seem that at Harrow Hill the mollusca suggest the presence of possible damp woodland and/or scrub, but also with grassland species represented (*Carychium* and *Pomatias* sp respectively), perhaps indicating an initial woodland setting with increasing clearings. Similar molluscan faunas were identified at both Blackpatch and Long Down, again tentatively implying at least a partially wooded habitat. The evidence from Grime's Graves contrasts with the South

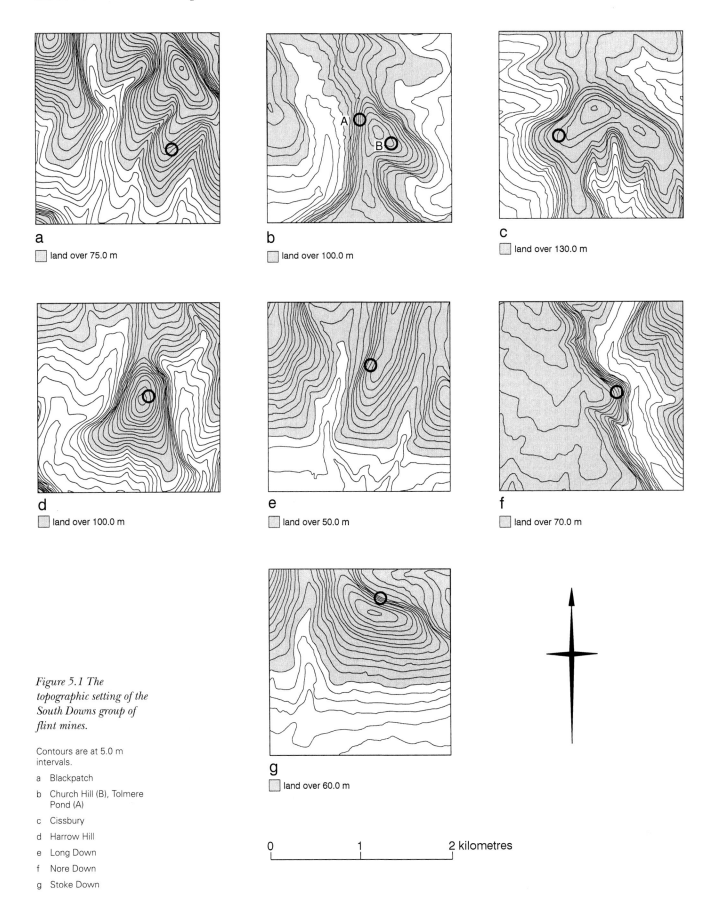

a

☐ land over 75.0 m

b

☐ land over 100.0 m

c

☐ land over 130.0 m

d

☐ land over 100.0 m

e

☐ land over 50.0 m

f

☐ land over 70.0 m

g

☐ land over 60.0 m

Figure 5.1 The topographic setting of the South Downs group of flint mines.

Contours are at 5.0 m intervals.

a   Blackpatch

b   Church Hill (B), Tolmere Pond (A)

c   Cissbury

d   Harrow Hill

e   Long Down

f   Nore Down

g   Stoke Down

0   1   2 kilometres

Downs and Wessex sites. There, the mines appear to have been located within more open woodland (Evans *et al* 1981), which considering the topography of the site suggests that visibility cannot have played much of a role in the choice of where to mine.

Site location

In recent years there has been increased consideration of the landscape vista both to and from prehistoric monuments. Viewsheds of barrows, for example, are considered to be an important aspect of their landscape positioning (eg Woodward and Woodward 1996). However, such approaches generally consider sites in their developed phase when all the components were in position. The few proven mines demonstrate an unsurprisingly limited range of landscape locations. Some are in quite prominent skyline positions, when observed from particular directions, such as Cissbury and Harrow Hill. Others, although located on high ground, occupy more locally restricted viewpoints, such as Long Down and the potential site at Nore Down. The remainder are relatively hidden by the more subtle topography, as at Grime's Graves and Buckenham Toft.

The South Downs group is situated along the downland between Worthing in the east (Cissbury)

and Havant in the west (Nore Down) (Figure 5.1). The eastern group of sites (Cissbury, Church Hill, Blackpatch and Harrow Hill) are roughly equidistant, separated from each other by around 2 km. At present, they demonstrate a degree of intervisibility, although only from Church Hill can the whole group be observed. In the Neolithic, we might envisage a more complex situation regarding intervisibility, dependent somewhat on local tree cover and also on the scale and extent of the mining earthworks at any given time. Cissbury is located on a south-west-facing downland summit extending to a little below the false crest; Church Hill lies upon a south-east-facing shoulder again from the summit to the false crest; Blackpatch is sited similarly to Church Hill but on a south-west-facing slope; and Harrow Hill is situated upon a north-facing downland summit and false crest (Figure 5.2). The aspect of visibility (either the view to or view from, or both) may have been a desirable attribute which served to highlight the significance of these places. Cissbury, Blackpatch and Church Hill may all have been visible from the coastal plain, whereas Blackpatch and Harrow Hill are hidden from it. On a clear day, and with favourable vegetation cover, the Isle of Wight can be seen from Cissbury.

The western group of sites on the South Downs are far less clustered. Some 10 km separates Long Down from Stoke Down, and 6 km lies

Figure 5.2 The mine site at Blackpatch seen from Harrow Hill. Available chronological evidence is poor but it seems likely that both sites overlapped to a degree. The question of intervisibility in the Neolithic is dependent on several unknown factors, including tree cover, and need not have been important. (AA96/2856)

between Stoke Down and Nore Down. These sites consequently lack intervisibility, but also appear to occupy a similar range of landscape locations. From Long Down, located upon the false crest of the western side of a valley, which runs north–south and overlooks the coastal plain, a series of Neolithic enclosures may have been visible. Court Hill lies 4 km to the north-west; Barkhale is 5 km to the north-east; and the possible Neolithic enclosure on Halnaker Hill is just 1 km to the west. However, dating evidence is poor for all four sites, making any discussion of intervisibility and inter-relationships highly speculative. Stoke Down is located upon the false crest of a north-east-facing ridge, which is only partly hidden from the coastal plain, but from which the causewayed enclosure on St Roche's Hill, beneath the Trundle hillfort, is likely to have been visible some 5 km to the east-north-east. Nore Down, meanwhile, is situated within a relatively secluded

valley on the false crest of an east-facing hillslope, which is completely hidden from the coastal plain and from which no known Neolithic sites could have been visible.

The Wessex group (Figure 5.3) displays some broad similarities with the South Downs group in terms of general location on the chalk downland, but some notable differences are also evident. None of the known mines are intervisible, although there are other broadly contemporary sites in close proximity to all of them. Martin's Clump is situated upon an east-facing false crest, overlooked by more prominent downland. A long barrow lies no more than 150 m to the south, and bearing in mind the single radiocarbon date from the mine (Figure 1.2; Appendix 2), the barrow may have been constructed while mining was occurring. At Easton Down, the mines are located at the head of a re-entrant with restricted views, apart from down the valley, or of the immediate

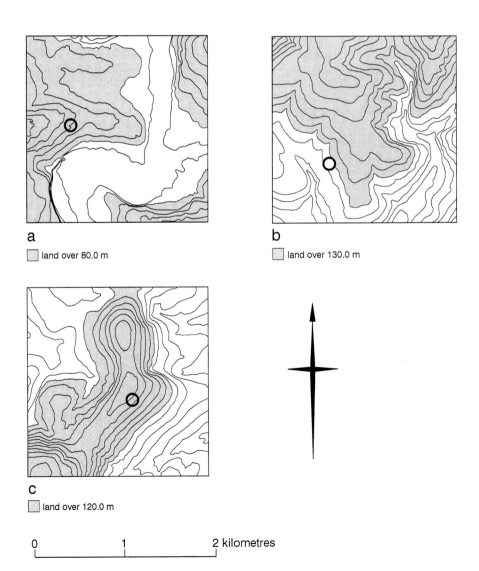

a

☐ land over 80.0 m

b

☐ land over 130.0 m

Figure 5.3 The topographic setting of the Wessex group of flint mines.

Contours are at 5.0 m intervals.

a Durrington Walls

b Easton Down

c Martin's Clump

c

☐ land over 120.0 m

0   1   2 kilometres

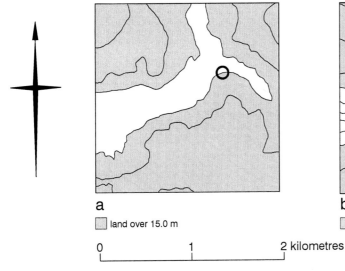

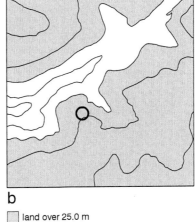

a

☐ land over 15.0 m

b

☐ land over 25.0 m

0   1   2 kilometres

Figure 5.4 The topographic setting of the Brecklands group of flint mines.

Contours are at 5.0 m intervals.

a   Buckenham Toft

b   Grime's Graves

downland. The few pits at Durrington, although rather imprecisely dated, were located on a south-east-facing false crest roughly 300 m to the north-east of the Durrington Walls henge, while the prominent Beacon Hill, a little to the east, was ignored. The presence of these pits may further highlight the long-term significance of the area evident in the building of the henge. Apart from Cissbury and Harrow Hill, where there is a choice of dramatic landscape position it is frequently disregarded.

The Breckland sites are located in a totally different topographic setting of more subtle rolling heathland (Figure 5.4). Grime's Graves is situated upon the north-facing side of a shallow dry valley aligned roughly east–west and leading into the Little Ouse catchment. Buckenham Toft, just 6 km or so to the north-north-east of Grime's Graves, occupies a similar setting in the valley of the River Wissey, which flows into the Great Ouse. These sites would seem to have had much less potential to utilise dramatic topographic locations. However, the exploitation of the flint strata may again have had more significance than just the availability of raw material. The ubiquitous presence of surface flint at these sites (information from F Healy) would suggest that mining was unnecessary for basic raw materials, yet it was the deeper, more hard-won floorstone that was the focus of much of the mining.

From the above, and bearing in mind both the requirement for flint to be present and the small number of sites we are dealing with, there seem to have been two basic locations for flint mines. Firstly, there are those in prominent locations, with a high degree of visibility to and from the sites. Secondly there are more discrete complexes relatively hidden from view either by vegetation, topography or both. For the first group, some comparison might be made with certain stone axe 'factories' such as Great Langdale (Bradley and Edmonds 1993) or Creag Na Caillich (Killin) (Edmonds *et al* 1992), which occupy very conspicuous locations on or near the skyline.

The downland mines are less dramatic vertically and their prominence more localised. Indeed, at the genesis of the mines such siting is likely to be fortuitous and based on previous activities within the landscape. It may be that their location close to the Clay-with-flints downland capping may have had some significance. This situation would have encouraged a dense woodland vegetation, contrasting with a more open woodland on the lower slopes off the Clay-with-flints, thus creating an increasingly prominent vegetation marker to these locations. Additionally, erosion at the edges of this capping may have encouraged tree-fall, thus producing a highly visible division between the two woodland zones and enhancing the strikingly verdant and dense covering to the downland tops.

The local visibility of certain mines on the South Downs may have been further enhanced by the apparent 'tilt' of their location, giving the impression that the mines lie obliquely when viewed from positions some distance away, rather than along the contours when viewed face-on. This factor, combined with the visual effects of clearings producing a 'notch' on the wooded horizons, may have guided the eye towards the mines when viewed from a distance. The location of the mines would also have been enhanced by

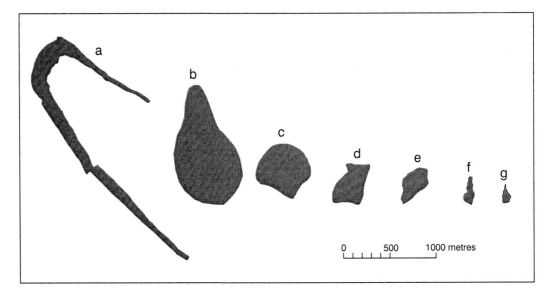

Figure 5.5 A diagram showing the relative areas of selected European flint mines in contrast to Grime's Graves and Church Hill.

a Krzemionki, Poland
b Świeciechów-Lasek, Poland
c Jablines, France
d Rijckholt, Netherlands
e Grime's Graves, England
f Ożarów, Poland
g Church Hill, England

Figure 5.6 (opposite) Aerial transcription of the flint mines at Stoke Down, West Sussex, showing the full extent of the complex. Note too, the attendant ring ditch, which is almost certainly a barrow, and the traces of 'Celtic' fields.

the whiteness of any recently placed chalk spoil dumps that had not grassed over. In this scenario the likely effects of woodland regeneration may have been of primary concern, and would necessitate some level of woodland management if the mines were required to remain visible. Such elements of heightened visibility might thus 'evoke memory' (Bradley 1993, 2) and help to maintain their role in the landscape at both local and interregional levels. However, where the mines are concerned, these are all aspects which are likely to have increased in significance as mining progressed, as the sites expanded and impacted on their surroundings, and as they became established in cycles of social activity.

The scale of the flint mines

Most of the English mines appear small when compared with many of the European sites (*see* Figure 5.5), ranging in area from *c* 0.5 ha at Nore Down (Figure 4.10), which has roughly eight recorded shafts, to Grime's Graves where at least 433 shafts occupy 7.6 ha (Figure 4.12). The earthworks at Martin's Clump (Figure 4.5) suggest that mining may have extended over roughly 8 ha and comprised as many as 1,000 small pits. Nearby at Easton Down (Figure 4.14), the area of activity covers some 16 ha but incorporates at least seventy much larger shafts. Stoke Down (Figure 5.6), meanwhile, has a more linear arrangement with traces of at least seventy shafts recorded as soilmarks ranged along a ridge for more than 750 m.

From the evidence of the new surveys, and allowing for variable amounts of disturbance in later periods, it does appear that in most cases the Neolithic flint mines were relatively compact when in use. Mining cannot have been an intensive activity when the number of recorded shafts is compared with the available radiocarbon chronology. At any given time, the number of shafts being exploited is likely to have been few, perhaps no more than one per year. In contrast, earthworks relating to later extraction processes, particularly the more recent gunflint industries, are often structurally different, isolated and widely spaced. The pits used by the miners at Lingheath, Brandon (Figure 3.1), for example, were at times uniformly arranged in rows. Even when irregularly spaced they were still at some distance apart in accordance with safety considerations and mining law. Direct comparison is difficult however. The economic concerns which motivated the gunflint industry will have been far removed from the social and cultural traditions that helped to structure exploitation of flint sources in the Neolithic.

The evidence for buildings at the mines

In England, Neolithic buildings are extremely rare in any context, and consequently it comes as no surprise that little evidence has been recovered for contemporary structures at the flint mines. On the South Downs, it has been suggested that no settlement was present in physical proximity to the mine shafts – the mines were primarily extraction and workshop sites where rough-outs were produced (Gardiner 1990, 121). Ethnographic examples hint at other culturally determined possibilities (*see* for example, Gould 1977; Flood 1983; Woolworth 1983; Matthiessen 1989). An important issue in this respect is the question of whether or not the mines were

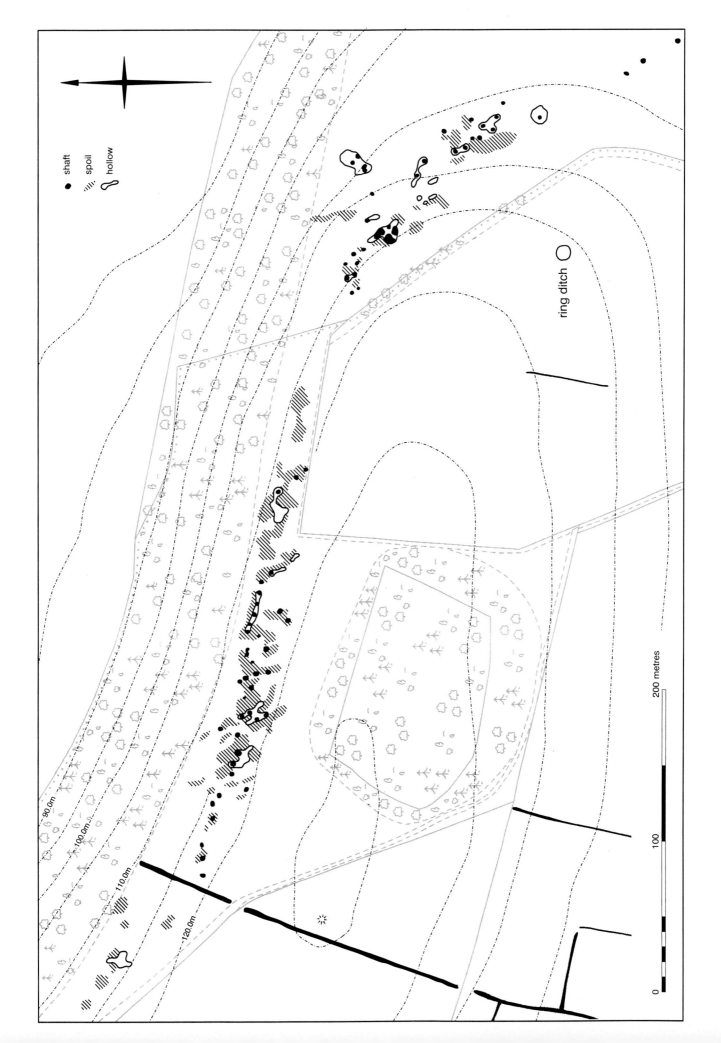

shaft
spoil
hollow

ring ditch

90.0m
100.0m
110.0m
120.0m

200 metres

100

0

utilised on an episodic, perhaps seasonal, basis, a factor which would clearly influence the nature and permanence of any structures at these places. If the mines were exploited by different mobile groups on an irregular basis or even a single mobile group on a seasonal basis, they might be expected to leave behind comparatively little structural evidence, although a question mark remains over the amount of cultural debris one might expect to be left behind.

There are two major factors to consider. First, and most obvious, the sampling bias inherent within the archaeological record has arisen from excavation strategies which have focused upon the most visible aspect of mining – the shafts themselves. The wider context of the mines has rarely been considered except in terms of the subsequent dispersal of flint mine products. The technology of mining and the typology of flint tool assemblages have underpinned most research. The second consideration is the potentially damaging effects of the original mining process on the survival of adjacent sites or features. Mining was a dynamic activity. Shafts were excavated, flint extracted, spoil deposited, then new shafts were dug, and the process repeated. The surface area of the mine complexes would have been in a state of periodic change as new shafts were sunk and new spoil dumps developed over different areas. Thus, not only is there a problem of sampling bias in excavation strategies, but the miners themselves could have been responsible for masking evidence of non-mining activity. The debris from hearths, the animal bones and the potsherds recovered from shafts and spoil heaps may be all that remains of contemporary activity within or around the mines.

Of course, it is not purely 'domestic' structures that might have existed. At Harrow Hill, excavations near the lip of shaft 13 recorded a series of circular or sub-circular depressions, two of which were 'deep and quite steep-sided' (McNabb *et al* 1996, 28–9), but their function remains uncertain. Their location suggests a number of possibilities. They could represent some form of winching structure; part of an earlier building, perhaps a workshop or house; or some form of mine shaft cover, perhaps of conical form designed to prevent flooding of the galleries. Evidence for such roofing over shafts has been discovered at Krzemionki in Poland (W Borkowski and W Migal pers comm; Borkowski 1997, 46–7), and is the type of feature that might be required for year-round exploitation of the mines. The ephemeral nature of post-built structures may well have made them difficult for earlier excavators, both at Grime's Graves and on the South Downs, to identify. It is worth noting that the present survey of Grime's Graves recorded several level platforms

situated between shafts, which could have held structures, and similar features were found at Harrow Hill.

At Blackpatch, Pull (1932, 52–4; Pull and Sainsbury 1929) recorded the occurrence of animal bones, flint implements and burnt material which could represent a broader range of activity at the site than purely flint extraction. Their presence in the upper fills of shafts could, however, be explained in several ways, and it is difficult to determine whether these deposits simply represent dumps of domestic detritus which accumulated during or after mining; or whether they represent the remains of activity including the preparation and consumption of meals during mining episodes; or if they represent more formal deposits, albeit on a smaller scale, of the sort undertaken at the broadly contemporary causewayed enclosures. Pull identified no physical structures among the mine shafts, but he did investigate a number of features which lay a short distance to the east, scattered over the shoulder of the ridge. Here, a large number of roughly circular shallow depressions, no more than 9 to 18 in (0.22–0.46 m) in depth and ranging from 8 to 20 ft (2.4–6.1 m) in diameter, were excavated. Their appearance as earthwork features was crucial in their recognition by Pull. No indications of hearths or postholes were recorded by Pull, but the primary silts within these features did contain assemblages of artefacts which were broadly contemporary with the mines. These comprised flint tools and flakes, broken sandstone rubbers, animal bones, burnt flints and a flint axe, plus some sherds of indeterminate pottery. The flint assemblage included a cache of six scrapers on the floor of one of these depressions. Unfortunately, only the briefest details survive of these features and there are no plans, sections or photographs. Their nature and date remain at best uncertain.

At nearby Church Hill, however, Pull was responsible for one of the few attempts to explore systematically the immediate environs of a flint mine. He opened an 'enormous number of trial holes and sections … over an area of nearly half a square mile in the vicinity of the shafts' (Pull 1935), perhaps influenced by the work being carried out by Armstrong at Grime's Graves. He originally identified a 'widely scattered group of small ill-defined depressions' a short distance to the north-west of the main flint mine complex which he initially regarded as 'dwelling pits' or 'hut sites'. These were not referred to subsequently by Pull, perhaps reflecting a change of heart over their interpretation.

Taken together, the evidence from the English mines for activity beyond the recovery and working of flint is difficult to evaluate. Chronological and physical relationships are elusive and detail is often poor. Of course we may be looking for signs of something that did not exist. If mining was an irregular seasonal activity, involving brief episodes of extraction, with any subsequent processing taking place away from the mines, then there would be little reason to expect more than the most ephemeral traces of structures and 'domestic' debris. This was a time when only the most transient remains survive of the places where people actually lived.

Other activities at the mines

Among the excavated evidence occur certain finds and features which offer an insight into how the mines were used and perceived beyond their obvious role as a source of raw material. It is clear that the English mines contain evidence for a range of activities which illuminate everyday social and ritual aspects of the extraction process (Figure 5.7). Some of these have already been touched on above in the search for traces of contemporary settlement. The evidence includes hearths which do not seem well placed for lighting or cooking purposes, although of course alternative functions can be suggested such as the provision of warmth or ventilation, or the heating of antler picks. More intriguing are apparently placed deposits of pottery, antler picks, animal bones and human skeletal material. Then there are occurrences of 'graffiti' and unusual axe markings on the chalk walls of galleries and shafts. Arguably, all of these could be tied in to the extractive process, but taken together they indicate that the recovery of flint was perceived as more than a simple process of raw material extraction.

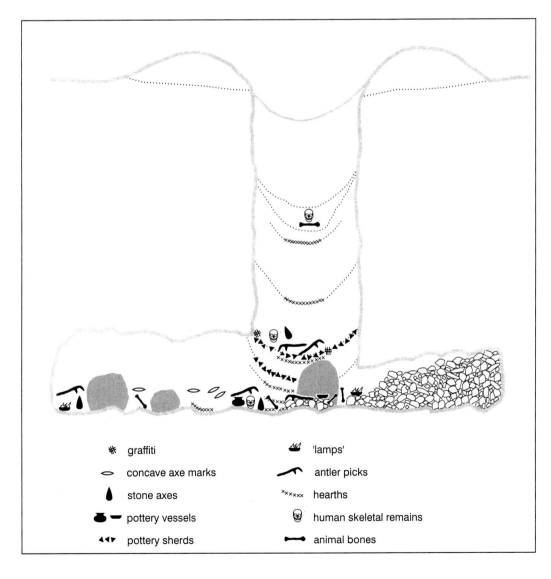

Symbol	Legend		Symbol	Legend
※	graffiti		⚓	'lamps'
⬭	concave axe marks		⌒	antler picks
⬤	stone axes		××××	hearths
⬤—	pottery vessels		☠	human skeletal remains
◄◄►	pottery sherds		⬤—	animal bones

Figure 5.7 Diagram illustrating the general distribution of artefacts and deposits in the English flint mines. Continuing deposition in the shaft fills should be noted.

Evidence from the shafts

The stratigraphic sequences recorded in the fills of many excavated flint mine shafts are at best ambiguous, reflecting in many cases the contemporary standards of archaeological excavation and recording. It has been suggested that many show little evidence of weathering (Holgate 1991, 15–17), which might imply that they were promptly backfilled. However, at Cissbury for example, the sections of at least two shafts (including the so-called 'Cave Pit' (Park Harrison 1878, 414)) along with others at Blackpatch suggest that weathering had in fact occurred, and that erosion was at least partly responsible for their backfill. Similar events were recorded at Grime's Graves where the stratigraphy in Pit 1 suggests that some galleries had been purposefully backfilled, but that erosion may have been responsible for the deposition of the basal layers within the shaft (layers VIIIA, VIII and IX). A slightly more complex sequence can be observed in Pit 2 (Clarke 1915b, fig 7), where the galleries may have been abandoned and left partly open, following which erosion has deposited a fine layer of chalk wash (layer VIII) that eventually sealed the gallery openings. Overlying this is a dump of chalk debris (layer V) that partly fills the base of the shaft and was presumably derived from an adjacent, and subsequent, shaft.

Both shaft sequences demonstrate that even after some initial backfilling, up to two-thirds of the depth of each shaft remained open until being filled by a series of distinctive deposits derived from various phases of mining in the immediate vicinity. In addition, the presence of bats in certain galleries, such as 1 and 8 at Pit 1 (Clarke 1915b, 55, 58) and 1, 3, 5 and 6 at Pit 2 (Clarke 1915b, 90), confirms that they were indeed open and quiet enough to be colonised by these timid creatures. Their presence also offers a further indication of seasonal exploitation. However, silting would have been a considerable problem if the shafts were left open intentionally. This is clearly illustrated by the re-excavation of Pit 1 at Grime's Graves in 1920, some six years after its original investigation. It was found that 2.5 m of silt had built up in the base of the shaft (Armstrong 1921), though visitor erosion may have been of significance. Nonetheless, such processes do have implications for the visibility of placed deposits and graffiti once extraction had ceased within a particular shaft.

Excavated evidence also suggests that shafts continued in use as foci for various activities during the backfilling process. For example, at Pit 1 at Grime's Graves, a hearth was identified in layer 9 on what was probably the primary silting near the base of the shaft (Clarke 1915b, 51). Various layers higher up the shaft fill contained potsherds and flint implements. Then, layer 5, located midway up

the shaft, was composed of chalk and floorstone debris either from an adjacent shaft or collapsed from a spoil dump. Within it was a human skull wedged between chalk blocks and lying immediately above an ox bone (Clarke 1915b, 48–9 and 69). Similar events occurred during the filling of Pit 2 (ibid, 72, 79–80), where a sequence of hearths was found down to a depth of 20 ft (6 m), as well as what may have been a later and intrusive inhumation. Such evidence is best recorded at Grime's Graves, which is also of course significantly later than the other dated mines, but episodic activity during shaft filling is also evident at sites such as Blackpatch and Church Hill.

Human remains from mine shafts have also occasionally involved more than the odd bone. One skeleton was discovered in Shaft VI at Cissbury, some 16 ft (4.8 m) below the surface, surrounded by chalk blocks and facing towards the east (Figure 5.8). Lying around the skeleton were six small flint tools, plus a flint axe placed near the knees, eight snail shells, a chalk disc, and a pebble marked by burning (Park Harrison 1878, 431). The body was that of a male, estimated by Rolleston to be roughly 25 to 30 years old (ibid, 431). Mining debris lay under the body, and the lower jaw of an ox came from roughly the same level in the shaft fill (Rolleston 1879, 381). 'No. 1 escarp shaft' at Cissbury contained a female skeleton found head down, the skull some 2 ft 6 in (0.76 m) above the floor level of the shaft (Lane Fox 1876, 375). Rather than representing deliberate burial, the excavator suggested that this might be an accident victim, eloquently demonstrating the dangerous nature of the flint mines. A further possible accident victim was encountered during Pull's excavations at Cissbury (Pull archive, Worthing Museum & Art Gallery). On the floor of a shaft was a female skeleton with a broken spinal column (though it is unclear in Pull's notes if this breakage is likely to have occurred before death). The skeleton lay on its side near the wall of the shaft, facing into the galleries. Charcoal was reportedly found in one hand.

Taken as a whole, the evidence for deliberate or accidental burial at the mines and broadly contemporary with mining is slight. The same goes for the presence of fragmentary human remains, the use and deposition of which is so well attested at causewayed enclosures in the earlier Neolithic, and at some henges and other monuments in the later Neolithic. Some remains appear to represent careful positioning and deliberate placing; others might have arrived at their final resting place by accident. In the case of whole bodies – the possible accident victims – it may have been both easier and more appropriate to leave them where they fell, and to allow backfilling to occur,

naturally or otherwise, around them. Finally, the fact that two of the three skeletons found deep in shafts at Cissbury were female is worthy of note.

The base of the shafts

Again, in terms of quality and quantity, the evidence is dominated by but by no means confined to Grime's Graves. Hearths have been recorded in many contexts, most notably throughout the lowest layers at Grime's Graves (Greenwell's Pit (Greenwell 1870), Pit 1 (Clarke 1915b, 42, 51–3), Pit 2 (Clarke 1915b, 72)) and at Cissbury ('Cave Pit' (Park Harrison 1878, 420)). Although these are generally not closely dated, their position within the shafts links them to the phases when access to the shaft bottom and galleries was still possible.

The hearths located upon or close to the shaft floors are of most interest. In Pit 1 at Grime's Graves, three were recorded in layer 10, near to the bottom of the shaft; hearth number 3 sealed a deposit of antler tines (Clarke 1915b, 51–2). In Pit 2, hearths were discovered on the floor of the shaft, one opposite the entrance to gallery 6, and another associated with flint artefacts and burnt

antlers (Clarke 1915b, 81). At the 'Cave Pit', Cissbury, a hearth enclosed by chalk blocks was recorded opposite the entrance to gallery B with blackened or burnt antler found nearby (Park Harrison 1877b, 435). In the 1971 shaft at Grime's Graves a further hearth was recorded in the centre of the shaft, surrounded by a scatter of nineteen antler picks (Mercer 1981a, 26, fig 13). The location of such hearths at the base of shafts argues against their use for the provision of light (during daylight hours at least) as this is one of the best-illuminated positions. The question of warmth might seem unlikely, as this would only have been necessary in the winter months, when the mines would have been more dangerous places to work anyway. Furthermore, the presence of bat roosts at Grime's Graves suggests that this was exactly the period of the year when the mines were at their quietest. Some have suggested that the fires were used for fire-hardening antler picks (Clarke 1915b, 53), and certainly there is good evidence from Grime's Graves that this did occur (Clutton-Brock 1984, 26). Whether this activity needed to take place at the base of the shaft is another matter, however.

Figure 5.8 The burial discovered by Lane Fox at Cissbury. Surrounding the skeleton is an arrangement of chalk blocks. A flint axe lies adjacent to the knees. Reproduced by courtesy of the Sussex Archaeological Society.

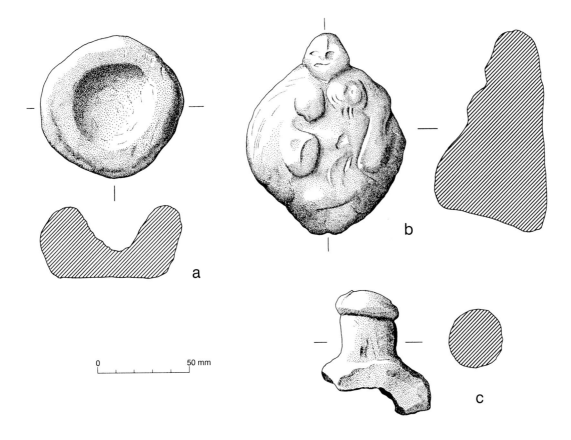

0   50 mm

Figure 5.9 Carved chalk objects found at Grime's Graves, comprising a chalk lamp (a), the 'Goddess' (b) and a phallus (c). After Longworth and Varndell 1996. © Copyright The British Museum.

Problems similarly beset the interpretation of the carved chalk 'lamps' (Figure 5.9a) recovered from many shaft floors, and sometimes from outer galleries such as Pit 2 at Grime's Graves. Reflected light illuminates many galleries for some distance beyond the base of the shafts, thus reducing the need for artificial light. In addition, there is no apparent evidence for burning associated within these objects (information from G Varndell), and none of the mines has produced convincing evidence of soot markings on the ceilings or walls of galleries, Consequently, the role of these little cup-shaped chalk artefacts remains obscure.

The so-called chalk 'platforms', comprising amorphous deposits of chalk blocks extracted from the mines, are also a frequent occurrence. To a certain extent these represent secondary deposits of mining debris whose removal from the shaft would have been both complicated and unnecessary. However, some platforms were also apparently utilised. Perhaps the most discussed is that found by Armstrong in Pit 15. It was composed of chalk blocks, and seven antler picks had been laid upon it and surrounded by a chalk cup, a chalk phallus, the carved chalk 'goddess' and flint nodules, and also featured a hearth on its north-eastern side. Doubts over the authenticity of the 'goddess' (information G Varndell; *see* Figure 5.9b) inevitably raise questions about the remainder of the deposit. However, in the shaft excavated in 1971 lay a similar platform upon which were a small hearth, a spread of debitage and the fragmented remains of two internally-decorated Grooved Ware bowls (Mercer 1981a, 24, fig 11). The prominent location of these bowls suggests that they were placed where they could not have been easily ignored: they may have encapsulated and communicated specific information to those entering or leaving the galleries. Alternatively, they may have represented the final act prior to abandonment of shaft and galleries. Considering the currency of Grooved Ware in henges and other sites, it may be that the message imparted by these vessels and the act of placing them had a far wider context than simply an association with mining. Other styles of Grooved Ware with less unusual or elaborate decoration were also found placed at the entrances to certain galleries, such as gallery 10 in Pit 2, where sherds with cord impressions were also recorded (Clarke 1915b, 210; Longworth *et al* 1988, 16).

Platforms have also been recorded at the earlier South Downs sites. At Blackpatch, the base of Shaft 1 featured a deposit of charcoal lying on a platform. A flint axe was nearby and adjacent to the entrance to gallery 5. Fragments of pig skull were recorded lying to the south-west, and another broken axe from the shaft floor completed the assemblage. The 'Cave Pit' at Cissbury featured a platform with a group of antler tines lying upon it (Park Harrison 1878, 421–2), that was adjacent to a feature interpreted as a hut or 'cave', which gave the shaft its name. This curious structure is so far unique among excavated mines. It was constructed of chalk blocks that enclosed an area of 7 ft by 5ft 6 in (2.1 m by 1.6 m), which appear to have abutted the walls of the shaft and rose up to meet an overhang, thus creating an enclosed space. An entrance on the east side was subsequently blocked and a new means of access cut through the chalk to link with the adjacent Shaft 1. The purpose of the 'cave' is unclear, but its juxtaposition to a chalk platform and a hearth might suggest some functional association between these features.

Evidence from the galleries

Many of the excavated English mines contain galleries extending from the base of the shafts. As with the floors of the shafts, these galleries were also the location for a variety of activities and deposits that do not readily fit into modern notions of extraction processes. Not all galleries remained open following the abandonment of a particular shaft. Some were partially or wholly backfilled with mining spoil, derived in the main from other galleries. In Pit 1 at Grime's Graves only gallery 1 was open at the time of abandonment (Clarke 1915b, 53), and contained a sequence of three hearths lying upon the accumulated debris within the gallery. At Pit 2 only galleries 1, 2 and 4 remained accessible out of the eight radiating from the base of the shaft (ibid, 83). A graffito was discovered between the entrances to galleries 4 and 7 – the so-called 'Tally Marks' (ibid, 74; *see* Figure 5.10a). This consisted of a crude lattice pattern, not dissimilar to those recorded from earlier Neolithic contexts on the South Downs, such as the 'Cave Pit' (Figure 5.11) and the 2nd Escarpment Shaft at Cissbury (Park Harrison 1877b, 434; Park Harrison 1877a, 266), or Nos 1 and 6 and 'Chessboard' from A–D III Harrow Hill (Curwen and Curwen 1926, 121–3; Curwen 1936, 86); and the chalk plaques discovered at causewayed enclosures such as Whitehawk (Curwen 1936, 86) and the Trundle (Curwen 1929, 61). Closer in date to Grime's Graves is the Grooved Ware bowl from Tye Field, Lawford (Shennan *et al* 1985, 173; *see* Figure 5.11). Such examples illustrate the apparently lengthy currency of a style of design utilised on both permanent sites and portable artefacts, and again draws the flint mines into a wider context of contemporary traditions and practices.

A second graffito in Pit 2 at Grime's Graves was positioned on the southern side of the arched entrance to gallery 6, some 7.5 ft (2.2 m) above the floor and overlooking a platform of chalk rubble and sand (Clarke 1915b, 73–4). This was named 'the Sundial' by the excavator, who noted that this series of linear striations (*see* Figure 5.10b) was lit by sunlight at noon. The significance of this is uncertain, but the positioning of the graffito above the platform is also worth highlighting. Overall, the positioning of graffiti at sites such as Cissbury, Harrow Hill and Grime's Graves, between or above the entrances to galleries, may have been intended to impart information about those galleries to anyone entering the shaft.

Figure 5.10 Graffiti from Grime's Graves, Pit 2, showing the 'Tally Marks' (a) and the 'Sundial' (b).

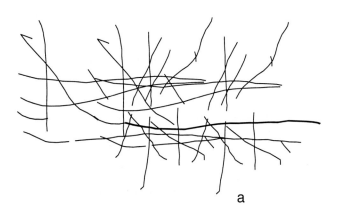

a

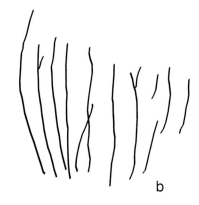

b

0   50 mm

Among the variety of unusual features to be encountered in galleries were marks made on the chalk walls by stone axes. Greenwell (1870) was the first to recognise such 'concave' markings at Grime's Graves (*see* Figure 2.3) in a gallery which also contained a ground axe, the possible cause of those markings (*see* p 7). Investigations at Cissbury did not recover similar markings, although three polished stone axes were found among the various galleries and shafts. Also at Blackpatch, excavations failed to recover traces of anything other than antler picks on the chalk walls (Pull 1932, 45).

Later excavations at Grime's Graves discovered further traces of ground axe marks in Pit 1, in galleries 2, 6, 7, 11, 13 (Clarke 1915b, 43) and possibly in gallery 12 (ibid, 59). Marks were also identified in Pit 2 between galleries 2 and 3 (ibid, 73), in gallery 11 (ibid, 85) and in gallery 5, where the marks occurred close to an axe of grey flint which lay beside a chalk lamp near the gallery entrance. Additionally, outside the shafts,

a further axe was recovered from Floor 15 (Peake 1917). Overall, very few ground axes have been recovered from Grime's Graves (Clarke 1915b, 157–8). The scarcity of ground axes from the mines might be considered surprising given the recorded presence of axe marks. They may well have been an efficient extraction tool; however, at the same time there is no reason why mining tools should simply be left abandoned at their place of use, something that raises questions about the quantities of antler picks left behind (Figure 5.12). Their placing in galleries and on shaft bottoms must have been among the last acts carried out within those places, as their presence would clearly inhibit any further activity in such confined spaces. Ethnographic studies have highlighted similar occurrences of tools being abandoned. For example, Flood (1983) describes how tools were left *in situ* so that the spirits were not displeased.

The use of the axes appears to have been limited in extent, perhaps confined to deliberately chosen places. In Pit 1, of the nineteen galleries in the complex, only nine featured axe marks. These are not located randomly on the walls of the galleries concerned. Four groups of marks were found on walls or buttresses radiating from all but one of the galleries at the base of the shaft. The other marks were all located where the gallery complex connected with other shafts to the north, east and south-west. This might suggest that the axes were used in places where their markings could be seen immediately upon entrance to the Pit 1 complex, and perhaps helped to define it as a unit. In Pit 2, the axe marks were placed in galleries leading from the shaft, or where they linked with other shafts. However, the presence of eleven marks within gallery 11 suggests extra significance for this location. The fact that two graffiti (the 'Sundial' and the 'Tally Marks') were also positioned in the base of the same shaft, at the entrances to two of the galleries, implies that a multiplicity of messages was being imparted about the use and definition of gallery complexes. Axes were being used for very specific purposes when taken down the mines, and in contrast to the antler picks, the usual mining tool, were rarely left behind (Figure 5.12).

Among the more unusual 'placed' deposits, recovered from excavated mines, was that found by Greenwell in one of the few galleries he examined. It comprised the skull of a phalarope (*Phalaropus* sp), a wading bird which is now a rare migrant to the British Isles (Jonsson 1992, 254). It lay between a pair of antler picks, the tines of which were facing inwards. A ground stone axe (Chapter 1 and above) lay at the base of the picks. As previously mentioned, the deposit was found in a gallery which featured the marks of a ground stone axe on its chalk walls (Greenwell 1870, 427;

Figure 5.11 Graffito from the 'Cave Pit' Cissbury, discovered during Lane Fox's excavations in 1876, and the Grooved Ware bowl with internal decoration from Tye Field, Lawford, Essex.

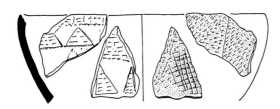

0   50 mm

Clarke 1915b, 17; Norfolk Record Office: 21198). The novel inclusion of the phalarope skull might represent some form of group or kinship affiliation with the mines. An interesting comparison with another Grooved Ware-associated site is provided by the presence of the remains of a white-tailed sea eagle at the Coneybury henge in Wiltshire (Richards 1990, 129 and 153).

Another unusual deposit associated with Greenwell's Pit but found during the British Museum's excavations over a century later occurred in gallery A/B. It consisted of the complete skeleton of a dog sandwiched between various dumps of chalk waste, which may have represented a specially constructed niche for the body. It is unlikely that the dog could have easily descended the 12 m deep shaft, or fallen down and crawled along the galleries to die. As the excavator has suggested, the animal was more likely to have died or been killed, either in the mine or elsewhere, before burial (Burleigh *et al* 1977, 357). An interesting parallel, again involving the remains of a dog, occurred at Easton Down (Stone 1935, 76–8).

Chronology and associated monuments

The problematic nature of the evidence for the chronology and duration of flint mining in England has already been touched upon (p 16). With the exception of Grime's Graves, the shortage of chronologically sensitive artefacts from secure contexts is compounded by the uneven quality and scope of the excavations undertaken at the various sites and their associated surviving archives and finds. As a result, discussions over dating have tended to rely principally on the available radiocarbon determinations (*see* Figure 1.2; Appendix 2). From these, two clear phases of Neolithic mining activity have been discerned (eg Mercer 1981a, 51; Gardiner 1990, 120; Bradley and Edmonds 1993, 37; Edmonds 1995, 51). Broadly speaking, an earlier Neolithic phase is represented by the West Sussex sites of Cissbury, Blackpatch, Church Hill, Harrow Hill and Long Down, and appears to be almost wholly contained within the 4th millennium BC. A second phase belongs to the 3rd millennium BC and includes the extraction at Grime's Graves and, possibly, Easton Down.

Figure 5.12 A cache of antler picks abandoned in Greenwell's Pit, Grime's Graves. (AA95/4951)

Some demonstrable differences do exist between the excavated sites contained within the separate phases in terms of mining technique, the range of lithic and ceramic material present, and the nature of the implements being created from the mined nodules. However, variation is also present within individual mining complexes, and it is unclear whether such differences alone, in the absence of radiocarbon determinations, could support any reliable phasing of the mines. Unfortunately, as has already been suggested, those determinations are themselves far from straightforward. Three of the mines (Blackpatch, Church Hill and Easton Down) are represented by single dates only. Along with Cissbury, they are represented by dates that were mostly obtained from material derived from poorly documented contexts and recovered during early excavations. In addition to the sizeable standard deviations, the problems recently outlined by Ambers (1996) concerning the accuracy and precision of many of the Grime's Graves results must be equally applicable to the Sussex and Wiltshire sites, as most of their dates were obtained during the same period and as part of the same dating programme. Long Down and Harrow Hill each has a series of dates derived from more recent excavation campaigns, although an absence of reliable dates from the other mines means that their value so far has been largely site specific. Furthermore, they suffer from another of the shortcomings associated with the dates from the other mines, namely that only a few episodes of activity have been sampled from what are clearly substantial, complex and long-lived sites.

These are problems which only the controlled excavation of samples from a variety of contexts at flint mines could hope to overcome. However, as a first step, during the course of this project, it became apparent that a number of potentially datable bone and antler artefacts from reasonably secure contexts survived from earlier excavations. Although many of the caveats outlined above would still apply to any fresh determinations, it was felt that the concerns held over the accuracy and precision of the previous results could at least be put to the test, and thus place the scientific dating of the South Downs mines on a slightly more secure footing. The British Museum's Department of Scientific Research kindly agreed to evaluate the identified samples, five of which ultimately proved suitable for radiocarbon assay using standard techniques (Figure 1.2, Appendix 2). Although two new dates from Harrow Hill do not overlap at the 95 per cent probability level, they do fall comfortably within the range indicated by previous determinations which had raised the possibility that mining at this site may have been underway during the late 5th millennium BC. However, these dates were primarily obtained from charcoal samples and their unreliability is highlighted by the fact that BM-2071R (4500 to 3810 Cal BC) – a charcoal sample from the basal fill of shaft 13 – barely overlaps with BM-2098R (3990 to 3370 Cal BC) – a sample obtained from elsewhere in the fill of shaft 13 – at the 95 per cent confidence level.

For Cissbury, BM-3086 also provides a useful confirmation of earlier dates, and has a much reduced error range, even though BM-3082 does not overlap with it at the 95 per cent level. As at Harrow Hill, both new dates provide a clear indication of mining activity at the site during the first half of the 4th millennium BC. The other mines in the Worthing–Findon group, Blackpatch and Church Hill, are still represented solely by a single date each, both obtained during the 1960s on antler samples excavated by Pull. Although the Church Hill date in particular is intriguingly early, little weight can be placed on it at present.

The pair of dates obtained from samples recovered by Holgate during his excavations at Long Down in 1984 fit into the pattern emerging from the other sites – that mining was occurring on the South Downs during the first half of the 4th millennium BC. However, it remains unclear quite how early mining began, or how long it continued. The new date for Martin's Clump, the first from that site, again offers a hint that mining may have been underway there prior to 4000 BC. However, the calibrated range makes an early 4th millennium date equally likely. Furthermore, it would be unwise to read too much into a single date. Nonetheless, it does underline the need to discover more about this site and its near neighbour at Easton Down.

Thus at best, the available radiocarbon dates can only point to a probability that mining or associated activities were occurring at particular periods. For the dated South Downs sites, it seems clear that there was mining activity during the first half of the 4th millennium BC, but on present evidence it is unclear how early that mining began, and how long after, say, 3500 BC it continued. In contrast, the numerous dates obtained from Grime's Graves suggest that mining there occurred almost wholly within the 3rd millennium BC. Artefact assemblages recovered from most mines are of little assistance in indicating the approximate periods of inception, duration and abandonment of each of the mining sites in question. In the case of several of the South Downs sites, the surviving excavation records suggest that mining and associated activities may well have continued beyond the date ranges inferred from the radiocarbon dates, but the situation is far from straightforward.

Despite a well-attested fondness of Neolithic populations for depositing substantial quantities of material culture into ditches or pits, the flint mines are notorious for lacking just this sort of material. At Grime's Graves, the Grooved Ware recovered from secure contexts within shafts confirms the chronological range of activity implied by the numerous radiocarbon dates obtained from the site. On the South Downs, the situation is more problematic. Artefactual support for 4th millennium BC mining at the Sussex sites is poor in both quality and quantity, although at the same time there is nothing directly contradictory among the surviving artefacts and documentation. Readily datable artefacts from secure contexts are few. A potsherd, recovered by Lane Fox at a depth of 13 ft (4 m), from within the fill of a shaft (according to its label) at Cissbury, has been identified as representing an earlier Neolithic carinated bowl, probably dating to the middle centuries of the 4th millennium BC (see Figure 5.13; eg Holgate 1995a, 133). However, its precise context and associations within the shaft fill remain uncertain. It may have represented activity which was either earlier than, or broadly contemporary with, the mining. Other artefactual assistance for the chronology of flint extraction is less secure. A rim sherd of later Neolithic Peterborough Ware was recovered from the ploughsoil along the eastern edge of the earthworks of the Long Down flint mine (Drewett 1983a; 1983b); its relationship to the mining remains uncertain. At Easton Down, Peterborough Ware is represented in the assemblage from pit B92 (Salisbury Museum 252/1933), although pottery from the excavations undertaken by Stone (1931a), and originally considered to be of 'Windmill Hill type', was briefly examined during the present study and is thought more likely to be Beaker. In neither case does there seem to be any direct connection with flint mining.

As if the material from the flint mines themselves was not problematic enough, discoveries from further afield have occasionally been offered as rather dubious supporting evidence for the dating of flint mining in southern England. At some considerable distance from the nearest mine is the unhafted flint axe found beside the Sweet Track in Somerset. Dendrochronology has demonstrated that the main phase of construction for the Sweet Track occurred c 3807/6 BC. The axe is therefore assumed to be of the same, or slightly later, date. According to Coles et al (1973, 289), 'a tentative assessment of the preliminary results suggests that the nearest source, Easton Down, provided the flint for the axe. If so, the date [of the Sweet Track] can be applied to the mine, but full confirmation is needed'. Subsequently, it has been stated (Hillam et al 1990, 218) that the axe 'has been identified as from one of the seams in Sussex, so the track date can be assigned to the mining operations in southeast England'. Notwithstanding the difficulties inherent in applying dates across such distances, the method used in sourcing the axe is unclear and apparently open to reinterpretation, while the basis for assuming that it was manufactured from mined flint is equally uncertain. In short, there is no evidence to confirm that the axe was made of mined flint, or that it came from either Easton Down or one of the Sussex mines.

Meanwhile, some sites have provided hints that mining on the South Downs may have continued into the 3rd millennium BC. Once more, however, the available evidence is far from ideal. Later activity focusing on these mine sites, in the form of barrows, enclosures and so on, will be noted later. At present, attention will focus upon Blackpatch and Church Hill, both of which are associated with burial monuments and other features which have yielded Collared Urns and Beakers from apparently secure contexts. These

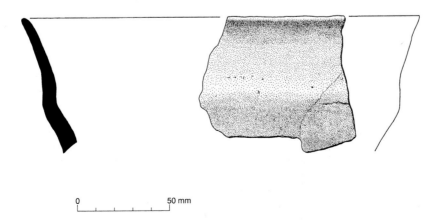

0   50 mm

Figure 5.13 An Early Neolithic 'Grimston Ware' bowl recovered from Lane Fox's excavations at Cissbury. It is now in the collection of the Pitt Rivers Museum, Oxford.

contexts have generally been regarded as representing activity that postdated the mining phase. Pull's archives and publications contain strong suggestions that there may have been an overlap – that some at least of this 'later' activity was in fact contemporary with flint mining. Unfortunately, the stratigraphical detail required to judge the issue properly is not available, meaning that considerable reliance has to be placed on Pull's fairly concise written descriptions and schematic plans and sections.

The main interest at Blackpatch focuses upon the presence of several monuments associated both with Collared Urns, which would suggest a date towards the end of the late 3rd millennium BC at the earliest, and with quantities of flint nodules. The latter occur mainly as a capping layer on several of the burial mounds, but are also present within the ditch of a nearby circular enclosure, sealing the primary silts throughout its whole circuit. Although Pull's notes suggest a close relationship between some mounds and the mines, this unfortunately does not apply to those containing Collared Urns, or other late material. For example, Pull's Barrow 12 was apparently partially overlain by spoil derived from one adjacent shaft, and was cut by another (Pull 1932, 84–7). The mound of Barrow 12 covered two crouched inhumations, one associated with a flint knife and a flint axe, and also contained the scattered remains of a third individual. While a Neolithic date seems perfectly plausible for these and several other burials at Blackpatch, it is unclear to what stage of the Neolithic they belong, particularly as they share certain characteristics with inhumations or cremations at the site which are accompanied by Collared Urns. It is unfortunate that no radiocarbon dates have been sought from surviving human skeletal material. Thus while it is clear that the mines at Blackpatch acted as a focus for funerary and perhaps other ritual/ceremonial activity into the early Bronze Age, possibly into the early 2nd millennium, a direct link between mining and this later material remains elusive. However, a problem that remains is the presence of the numerous (though unquantified) flint nodules forming a capping on some of the mounds, which require some explanation if, as Pull indicated, they represented mined flint.

After mining

Blackpatch is not alone among the flint mines, or other types of Neolithic sites or monuments generally, in providing considerable evidence for activities which differ from and postdate the primary phase of use. Backfilled shafts were widely utilised for the deposition of various forms of material, from the Beaker-associated cremation near the top of Shaft 1 at Church Hill (Pull 1933b) to the later, but considerable, deposits of Deverel-Rimbury pottery and associated material at Grime's Graves (see Longworth et al 1988; 1991). The latter site also offers the clearest indications of surface debris from the mining phase being used as a quarry for flint during later periods. Such recycling of spoil dumps has also been attested at certain stone axe factory sites, such as Langdale (R Bradley pers comm; Bradley and Edmonds 1993). Unfortunately, in all cases the chronological relationship between mining and later, non-mining activity remains uncertain. The burial monuments and other sites at Blackpatch, Church Hill and Grime's Graves suggest an importance beyond the utilisation of spoil as a raw material resource, while the presence of Grooved Ware at Church Hill (Wainwright and Longworth 1971, 287, no. 56) and of Beaker at sites such as Blackpatch (Pull 1932, 82) and Easton Down is of equally uncertain significance. The recovery of human remains from within shaft fill at Cissbury (Lane Fox 1876, 375–6) and the relationship of Barrow 12 to the mining at Blackpatch suggest that funerary and other activities may have been occurring while mining was still taking place. This, in combination with the 'later' material and the reuse of mining spoil may mean that it is inappropriate to think in terms of these sites falling out of use or being abandoned during or at the end of the Neolithic. Mining may have ceased, but other aspects of these sites may have developed in significance, and new uses and meanings may have arisen. Overall, the fragmentary strands of evidence do suggest that it may be too simplistic to expect the traditional chronological model to remain valid. Evidence is appearing or being reassessed, which is broadening both the possible date ranges for mining and the dichotomy between the dating of the South Downs group and those in the Breckland. It is also breaking down some of the clear lines that have been drawn between mining and other activities recorded from these sites.

At other South Downs sites, the situation presented by Pull at Blackpatch and Church Hill is less straightforward, either because neighbouring monuments have not been excavated or because, spatially at least, they are more distant from the mine earthworks. Cissbury, Stoke Down and the Wessex sites at Martin's Clump and Easton Down all feature round barrows in fairly close proximity. However, even if they clearly postdate the mines, it could be argued that the presence of the mines, whatever their contemporary status as a raw material resource, influenced the location of at least some of these monuments. Similarly suggestive is a feature observed during this survey at Grime's Graves. In the West Field, just 30 m north of the southern perimeter fence, lies a circular vegetation mark comprising a band of markedly darker green grass 2 m in width enclosing an area 19 m in diameter. A possible gap 2 m wide occurs on the east side. This may be a round barrow destroyed by the ploughing recorded during the survey, and if so its position would be of interest as it mirrors the location of the Grimshoe mound to the east of the mines (though *see* below).

Moving further through time, the situation becomes a little more difficult. The substantial deposition of Deverel-Rimbury material at Grime's Graves, associated with mixed farming settlement incorporating a specialised dairy economy (Legge 1992), is not mirrored at the earlier South Downs sites, although there are some suggestions that flint from some of the mines continued to be of significance. For example, an enclosure some 400 m west of the Blackpatch mines, and associated with Deverel-Rimbury pottery, had an enclosure bank revetted with tabular flint more likely to have come from a seam than to have been collected from the surface. Two circular depressions associated with it contained large quantities of flint, and appear to have been utilised for sporadic deposition until the Roman period (Ratcliffe-Densham and Ratcliffe-Densham 1953). It may be worth noting at this point the presence of a previously unrecorded and undated rectangular enclosure at Easton Down to the south of the mines which was observed during this survey. It is incorporated within a 'Celtic' field system but the chronological relationship is obscured as a result of later cultivation. Two depressions inside it may well be the sites of round houses rather than mine shafts. A sub-rectangular enclosure also exists as an earthwork within the northern part of the hillfort at Cissbury, and immediately to the east of the mines. It was excavated by Lane Fox and assigned a Neolithic date on the strength of flints recovered from the ditch (Lane Fox 1869b, 63). The enclosure is certainly earlier than the field system as a field bank abuts it, but its form would be unusual in a Neolithic context and it seems more likely that it overlies and cuts through Neolithic deposits.

It is not until the 1st millennium BC that any substantial activity is next attested at any of the mines. At Harrow Hill, at some point early in that millennium, possibly in the late Bronze Age, a sub-rectangular earthwork enclosure was constructed which overlapped with the flint mine earthworks. The excavations undertaken by Holleyman (1937) in particular suggest that to interpret the site as an enclosed settlement or a hillfort is a little simplistic given both the location and the nature of depositional activities attested there, the latter

apparently involving large quantities of cattle skulls (*see also* Manning 1995). At Cissbury, the construction of a major hillfort as well as extensive later prehistoric and Roman activity (including 'Celtic' fields) have obscured the surface traces of Neolithic mining and suggest that by this stage the mines had lost much of the significance they previously held as physical reminders of the past.

The occasional Roman potsherd has been recovered from topsoil or surface layers at some mines, but the next chronological phase represented at some mines occurs in the post-Roman period. At Blackpatch, some of the Neolithic and early Bronze Age burial monuments were used for the burial of Saxon inhumations, a number of them lacking skulls, and one featuring a substantial thigh wound. In addition, Pull's Barrow 10, assumed by him to be prehistoric (Pull 1932) may well have been constructed during this period (Welch 1983, 460). The mound was composed of soil and Clay-with-flints, rather than the mining spoil, flint nodules and knapping debris that characterised the other burial mounds. In addition, there is no indication that the male extended inhumation contained within a chalk-cut grave-pit beneath the mound was anything other than a primary interment. At nearby Harrow Hill, evidence for activity at this date is lacking, though the name is regarded as being suggestive of a pagan or heathen temple (Manning 1995). Whether this represents an Anglo-Saxon use or interpretation is less clear. At Grime's Graves, the Grimshoe mound is also of relevence for the later 1st millennium AD. Lying to the south-east of the mine complex and little more than 30 m within the perimeter fence, the mound is approximately 20 m in diameter and 2.2 m high. It appears to have been constructed on a plinth 0.7 m high, which may have been subsequently squared off by cultivation. The plinth in particular may originally have been spoil from an adjacent shaft, although it is not illustrated in the excavated section (Peake 1915, 110). Excavation within the mound revealed layers of boulder clay and red sand heaped against earlier tips of similar material, and a 'chipping floor' was recorded amongst these. Peake thought that the mound represented spoil overlying an earlier burial mound, but evidence for both the burial and its mound appears to be slight. In view of the fact that the mound represented the meeting place of Grimshoe Hundred (Blomefield 1739; Lawson *et al* 1981, 26), it is plausible that it was, at least in part, constructed in the later 1st or early 2nd millennium AD by scooping up material from the surrounding land surface. However, the name applied to both mound and mines suggests that by this time any awareness of the former use and significance of the site were long forgotten.

6
Conclusions

The information gathered during the course of this project from the new field surveys, the published literature, archival sources and museum assemblages, has offered the opportunity to reassess Neolithic flint mines. Several fundamental issues have emerged. Firstly, the scale of the individual mining complexes is small in comparison with many examples in Europe, such as Krzemionki in Poland (Borkowski 1995a; 1995b), Jablines in France (Bostyn and Lanchon 1992) or Rijckholt in the Netherlands (Clason 1981), each of which covers many hectares (*see* Figure 5.5). When the size of the English mines is considered in connection with the available chronological evidence – and in an English context the only detailed chronology is the later Neolithic series of radiocarbon dates from Grime's Graves – the numbers of shafts in comparison with the potential period of exploitation suggests that no more than one shaft per year may have been excavated. Amongst the earlier Neolithic sites of the South Downs and Wessex, the probability is that shafts were dug even less frequently. The mines may have been exploited on an episodic, perhaps seasonal basis, but whatever the true picture, mining appears to have been a small-scale enterprise.

It is clear that surface flint and material derived from outcrops during the Mesolithic had been of sufficient quality to produce large artefacts such as tranchet axes and 'Thames picks' (Care 1979), which are of comparable size to Neolithic axe types. Furthermore, identifiable mines do not appear to have existed in many areas that feature flint deposits, such as East Yorkshire, Lincolnshire, Dorset, Surrey and Kent, where surface deposits were utilised, illustrating a clear requirement for flint but without the need to mine for it. In addition, the presence of surface flint at almost all of the mine complexes observed during the present study demonstrates that raw material was readily available without the need to invest labour to sink a shaft. This leads to the conundrum that if there were adequate sources of flint available from surface deposits to manufacture even most large tool types, then why mine at all? Of course, the needs of the Neolithic differed from those of the Mesolithic, as forest clearings for agriculture and for timber became an increasingly important aspect of social and economic life. However, the evidence lends

weight to the implication that mining also served other needs, or was carried out because the flint obtained from such depths was imbued with symbolic value rather than being of purely practical importance. Again ethnographic studies provide a potential insight. For example, Gould (1977) recorded differences in perception between surface stone, which was discarded following use, and the curated stone obtained from quarries which were considered totemic, ancestral 'dreaming' places.

Recent studies (Gardiner 1984; Holgate 1988) have suggested that recognisably mined flint formed only a small proportion of the flaked stone assemblages from non-mining sites in southern England. Mined flint may also have been used predominantly for specific tool types: primarily axes in the earlier Neolithic and discoidal knives in the later Neolithic (Gardiner 1984, 28; Holgate 1988, 24), although overall, mined flint appears to have been used for a whole range of products. Even allowing for the effects of taphonomic processes and the difficulty of distinguishing mined flint from surface flint, patterns are beginning to emerge to support these specific correlations.

Aspects of the mining process required a high degree of technical competence and organisation, yet some of the small pits could have been dug by an individual in an afternoon. The physical remains of the extraction process range from small pits to massive, galleried shafts. At Grime's Graves, Sieveking (1979) has suggested that large, organised groups were responsible for arranging extraction via the large shafts, whereas the smaller pits might represent more *ad hoc* exploitation by local groups, perhaps at a family or kinship level. In Sussex, however, many of the smaller pits appear integral to the organised exploitation from the large shafts. It might be better to envisage a more fluid situation with social, cultural and economic factors determining the timing and extent of any episode of extraction and the number of people involved. Nonetheless, it may still be the case that the sinking of shafts and the recovery of flint nodules were activities requiring particular skills, and not necessarily involving the participation of the whole community. In this respect it is worth mentioning again the presence of female skeletons deep within shafts at Cissbury.

The location of flint mining complexes does not seem to have been a random process. Neither the best quality nor the most easily won flint is represented at several of the larger sites, suggesting that other factors helped to determine which particular flint resources developed into flint mines. The favoured sites may have had a long history of occasional and small-scale exploitation of surface or outcropping material, and as such have become an integral part of the resource and activity cycle of particular social groups. On present evidence, however, this is difficult to prove, although the landscape setting of some sites might argue in favour of their having fulfilled an important role in the social landscape prior to the occurrence of flint mining.

Arguably, therefore, mining was a specialised activity, its practice and its products imbued with a significance that extended beyond the merely utilitarian, although of course there can be little doubt that many of the products of flint mining were used to fulfil utilitarian needs. This emphasis towards a greater social significance for mined flint also helps to focus attention on the range of artefacts and other features recovered from the galleries and shafts. The placed deposits, the graffiti, structural features such as the chalk platforms and the carved chalk objects all begin to link the flint mines into a broader context of activities and traditions attested at contemporary monuments, such as the causewayed enclosures of the earlier Neolithic and the henges of the later Neolithic – all of which fulfilled a variety of functions to the communities who constructed and used them. The activities evident at the mines parallel depositional episodes not just at these other Neolithic monument types, but at sites and natural features throughout later prehistory. Although today, they appear somewhat unusual and out of place with what is often perceived as a purely extractive process, to the Neolithic miners the use and deposition of particular objects, and the performance of particular activities, may have been seen as an essential part of the mining process.

Some of the value of mined flint may well have lain in its aesthetic qualities, whether through its base colour or its patterning, a value which might have been heightened by knowledge of its source and the difficulties of extraction. The complexity of the extraction process, as seen also at the axe factory sites, perhaps coupled with socially controlled restrictions on access to the mines themselves, must have imbued the flint with deep symbolic value, which was heightened when fashioned into various artefact forms. This may have been particularly true for the axes through their role in woodland clearance for both agriculture and for timber to use in the construction of substantial funerary and ceremonial monuments. This creation of a definitive artefact, so closely linked to the maintenance of contemporary lifestyles, may in turn have contributed to the social significance of the mines themselves.

One of the most intractable problems remains the relationship of the flint mines to the patterns of settlement and exploitation of the surrounding landscapes. Even for the later Neolithic, traces of such activity tend to be ephemeral – pits and lithic scatters. The archaeology of the Neolithic in general remains dominated by the ceremonial and funerary monuments, to which we can of course add the monumental remains of certain extractive processes. The present study has resulted in new insights into the ways in which Neolithic communities might have perceived and exploited such sites, and provides a broader platform from which further work might put the flint mines into a wider social context.

Suggestions for further research

This project has provided the data for a considered synthesis of the flint mines of England, and during the course of fieldwork some areas requiring further research have become apparent. Firstly, there is a need for geophysical survey to create more complete records of plough-damaged mines than topographic survey alone can create, and also to test the periphery of surviving earthwork sites to establish their true limits. In addition, the use of geophysics might help to identify the presence of buildings or structures, which might help to inform future excavation strategies.

Many problems of interpretation can now only be answered by excavation. In particular, more work is needed upon the surface remains to determine whether buildings or settlement were present. The question of sequences of shafts also needs to be addressed, alongside an assessment of the range of mining techniques represented at the mines. Apart from Grime's Graves, chronology generally is very uncertain and there is scope for a more detailed dating programme, in addition to fieldwork that focuses particularly on the earlier stages of the mines in order to elucidate how they developed. A more robust palaeo-environmental programme analysing the full range of data, including palaeobotany and soil micromorphology, would provide a more useful and rounded picture of the environmental setting of the mines.

In terms of the dissemination of archaeological information, and particularly of the history of technology, only at Grime's Graves can the public begin to appreciate the achievement that the flint mines represent. There may be a case to be made for opening a similar shaft in Sussex so as to improve awareness and understanding of these internationally important monuments.

Appendix 1
Site Gazetteer

The following gazetteer focuses solely on those sites for which Neolithic flint extraction via the digging of vertical shafts – that is, mining – has been claimed or demonstrated. The first list contains the few sites at which mining has been demonstrated by excavation. The second mentions sites for which insufficient information prevents either confirmation or rejection. In some cases, such as Nore Down, interpretation as a flint mine seems likely, but has yet to proven by adequate excavation. In one case, Markshall, problems with access have prevented a proper assessment of the site. The third and final list comprises sites for which claims of Neolithic flint mining are almost certainly incorrect. However, inclusion in these last two lists does not rule out the possibility of prehistoric exploitation of a flint resource. In some cases, such as East Horsley, there had clearly been a considerable amount of lithic-related activity, but that activity appears not to have involved mining.

Each site entry is accompanied by the following information, where appropriate:

NGR: the Ordnance Survey national grid reference, providing an approximate location for each site to six figures.

NMR number: the unique reference number for each site within the National Monuments Record. This is the number that should be cited when requesting further details from English Heritage.

Excavations: a summary list of the principal known excavations at each site. Further details are held within the National Monuments Record.

Main published sources: a summary list of the principal published accounts of each site. Detailed lists of sources, including unpublished material, are held within the National Monuments Record.

Comments (lists (2) and (3) only): a brief summary of the reasons for either exercising caution, or discounting suggestions of flint mining.

1. Definite flint mines

Blackpatch, Patching, West Sussex (site plan, Figure 4.13)
NGR: TQ 094088
NMR number: TQ 00 NE 5
Excavations: Pull 1922–30
Main published sources: Goodman *et al* 1924; Pull 1932

Church Hill, Findon, West Sussex (site plan, Figure 4.7)
NGR: TQ 114083
NMR number: TQ 10 NW 46
Excavations: Willett late 1860s?; Pull 1932–52
Main published sources: Law 1927; Pull 1933a; 1933b; 1953; Holgate and Butler forthcoming

Cissbury, Worthing, West Sussex (site plan, Figure 3.5)
NGR: TQ 136079
NMR number: TQ 10 NW 4
Excavations: Irving *c* 1856; Lane Fox 1867; Lane Fox and Greenwell 1868; Willett 1873; Tindall 1874; Lane Fox 1875; Harrison 1876–8; Pull 1952–5
Main published sources: Irving 1857; Lane Fox 1869b; Willett 1875; Lane Fox 1876; Harrison 1877a; 1877b; 1878

Durrington, Wiltshire
NGR: SU 154440
NMR number: SU 14 SE 27
Excavations: Booth and Stone 1952
Main published sources: Booth and Stone 1952

Easton Down, Winterslow, Wiltshire (site plan, Figure 4.14)
NGR: SU 237359
NMR number: SU 23 NW 26
Excavations: Stone 1930–4
Main published sources: Stone 1931a; 1931b; 1933a; 1933b; 1935

Grime's Graves, Weeting with Broomhill, Norfolk (site plan, Figure 4.12)
NGR: TL 817898
NMR number: TL 88 NW 4
Excavations (selected): Greenwell 1868–70; Prehistoric Society of East Anglia 1914; Armstrong 1915–1939 intermittently; Mercer 1971–2; Sieveking/British Museum 1972–6
Main published sources: Greenwell 1870; Clarke 1915b; Armstrong 1927; 1934a; 1934b; Mercer 1981a; 1981b; Longworth *et al* 1988; 1991; Longworth and Varndell 1996; Sieveking 1979

Harrow Hill, Angmering, West Sussex (site plan, Figure 4.2)
NGR: TQ 081100
NMR number: TQ 01 SE 23
Excavations: Collyer *c* 1896; Curwen and Curwen 1924–5; Holleyman 1936; Sieveking 1982; 1984; Holgate 1984
Main published sources: Curwen and Curwen 1926; Holleyman 1937; Holgate 1995b; Holgate and Butler forthcoming

Long Down, Eartham, West Sussex (site plan, Figure 4.11)
NGR: SU 931093
NMR number: SU 90 NW 9
Excavations: Salisbury 1955–8; Holgate 1984
Main published sources: Salisbury 1961; Holgate 1985; Holgate 1995b; Holgate and Butler forthcoming

Martin's Clump, Over Wallop, Hampshire (site plan, Figure 4.5)
NGR: SU 252388
NMR number: SU 23 NE 5
Excavations: Stone and Clark 1933; Watson 1954–5; Fowler 1984
Main published sources: Stone 1933c; Fowler 1987; 1992

Stoke Down (West Stoke), Funtington, West Sussex (site plan, Figure 5.6)
NGR: SU 832096
NMR number: SU 80 NW 13
Excavations: Wade 1910–13
Main published sources: Wade 1922; Holgate and Butler forthcoming

2. Possible flint mines

Brading Down, Brading, Isle of Wight
NGR: SZ 599866
NMR number: SZ 58 NE 11
Comments: Field investigation was unable to confirm or reject suggestions of Neolithic flint mining. Struck flint occurs in profusion in the area, although there has been recent chalk quarrying. Flint seams here are almost vertical and would require different methods of extraction to those recorded from known flint mines. Any earthworks that may have existed have effectively been obscured by a 'Celtic' field system.

Buckenham Toft, Stanford, Norfolk (site plan, Figure 4.1)
NGR: TL 833949
NMR number: TL 89 SW 10
Main published sources: Greenwell 1870, 432; Clarke 1908, 116; Layard 1922, 491–2, 498
Comments: While the recent survey and the reports of Greenwell and Clarke cannot be regarded as conclusive, the possibility of Neolithic flint mining cannot be ruled out without further investigation.

High Wycombe, Buckinghamshire
NGR: SU 8693 (site unlocated)
NMR number: SU 89 SE 26
Main published sources: Anon 1902; Oakley 1902; Head 1955, 38
Comments: The available information, though brief and imprecise, certainly raises the possibility that flint mines existed.

Lynford (Swell Pit), Norfolk
NGR: TL 82859083
NMR number: TL 89 SW 17
Comments: Recent observation noted considerable evidence for gunflint working and gravel quarrying. However, information from Norwich County Museum suggests that there may have been a Neolithic element to the extraction.

Markshall, Caister St Edmund, Norfolk
NGR: TG 227048
NMR number: TG 20 SW 6
Main published sources: Clarke 1935, 356
Comments: A quantity of flint debitage has been recovered from the area and a circular depression has been reported. Access is difficult and an inspection of the site has not yet proved possible.

Nore Down, Compton, West Sussex (site plan, Figure 4.10)
NGR: SU 773131
NMR number: SU 71 SE 20
Excavations: Haslemere Archaeological Group 1982
Main published sources: Aldsworth 1983
Comments: Although the excavation was too limited in extent to be conclusive, the field survey evidence strongly supports identification of the site as a flint mine.

Norwich (Westwick St/Coslany St), Norfolk
NGR: TG 227088
NMR number: TG 20 NW 380
Main published sources: Holgate 1991, 10
Comments: The site could not be visited as it is
below street level. The extant evidence is
inconclusive – proximity to the water table and
the existence of chalk and flint quarrying in the
Norwich area in the historical period does not
preclude an earlier date for the observed features.

Slonk Hill, Adur, West Sussex
NGR: TQ 225066
NMR number: TQ 20 NW 89
Excavations: Hartridge 1969–74
Main published sources: Hartridge 1978
Comments: The excavation of the single pit was
too limited to be conclusive. Further
investigation is necessary to confirm
identification as a Neolithic mine shaft.

**Tolmere Pond (Tolmere Road), Findon, West
Sussex** (site plan, Figure 4.6)
NGR: TQ 110085
NMR number: TQ 10 NW 66
Excavations: Curwen and Curwen 1926; Pull
1949–50
Main published sources: Curwen and Curwen
1927
Comments: While some of the visible features
may represent the remains of Neolithic flint
mining, the excavations undertaken to date have
produced evidence that is at best inconclusive.
The lack of struck flint in the area and the
presence of a limekiln highlight the need for
caution. Further investigation is necessary.

Whitlingham, Kirby Bedon, Norfolk
NGR: TG 264077–TG 286078
NMR number: TG 20 NE 51
Main published sources: Halls 1908; Clarke
1912a, 165
Comments: Concentrations of knapping debris
and occasional finds of antler picks are reported
from the area, though there is also evidence for
recent flint and chalk quarrying. Prehistoric
activity may have focused on natural exposures
along the river bluff. A skeleton with antler(s)
was discovered here in a tunnel.

3. Discredited flint mines

Ashtead, Surrey
NGR: TQ 183575
NMR number: TQ 15 NE 21
Main published sources: Lowther 1943
Comments: Although some worked flints of

prehistoric date have been recovered, the pits
are broadly Iron Age or Roman in date.

Bacton, Edinthorpe, Norfolk
NGR: TG 306303
NMR number: TG 33 SW 65
Comments: Reports of large pits with dark infill.
However, the site is located on a valley floor, and
flints recovered often bear a distinctly
ferruginous patina, suggesting that flint from the
drift was being exploited. Observation saw no
evidence of pits in the area.

Badgerdell Wood, Chipperfield, Hertfordshire
NGR: TL 047035
NMR number: TL 00 SW 14
Main published sources: Castle 1971, 5
Comments: Unable to gain access to the site.
However, the reasons for identification are
uncertain, and Ordnance Survey field
investigation in 1975 found nothing to suggest
the presence of flint mines. The NGR falls within
an area of Clay-with-flints.

Baycombe Wood, Slindon, West Sussex
NGR: SU 966090
NMR number: SU 90 NE 144
Comments: A group of depressions on the false
crest of a slope, where nodular flint seams
appear to be close to the surface. Although the
siting is appropriate for Neolithic mining, the
depressions appear to represent more recent
quarrying. There is no evidence for Neolithic
exploitation.

Bow Hill, Stoughton, West Sussex
NGR: SU 824108
NMR number: SU 81 SW 22; SU 81 SW 46
Excavations: Hamilton 1933
Main published sources: Hamilton 1933
Comments: The morphology of the extant
earthworks and the presence of a trackway,
which clearly predates a number of the pits,
argue against a Neolithic date.

Chanctonbury Hill, West Sussex
NGR: TQ 1312 (precise location of alleged mine
uncertain)
NMR number: TQ 11 SW 78
Main published sources: Engelen nd
Comments: There is absolutely no evidence for
early flint extraction on Chanctonbury Hill,
although recent chalk quarries exist in the
general area.

Clanfield, Hampshire
NGR: SU 717159
NMR number: SU 71 NW 26
Main published sources: Cunliffe 1973; Engelen nd

Comments: Cunliffe's use of the term 'stone axe factory' seems to have prompted the inclusion of the site in Engelen's flint mine gazetteer, in which it is erroneously located in Huntingdonshire. The numerous flint finds from the area seem to represent exploitation of material within Clay-with-flints deposits.

Compton Down, Compton, West Sussex
NGR: SU 7614 (precise location uncertain)
NMR number: SU 71 SE 21
Main published sources: Drewett 1977; 1978; Aldsworth 1983
Comments: The possibility of a mine shaft existing on Compton Down was noted by Drewett during the late 1970s. However, he now considers the feature more likely to be a marl pit (Drewett, pers comm).

Cranwich, Norfolk
NGR: TL 769920–TL 779927
NMR number: TL 79 SE 5, TL 79 SE 11
Main published sources: Halls 1914
Comments: Although surface finds of prehistoric implements have occurred, the field evidence for mining is not convincing. Observation noted recent quarrying and probable marl pits.

Crayford, Kent
NGR: uncertain
NMR number: none assigned
Main published sources: Spurrell 1880; 1881
Comments: A denehole which contained some residual prehistoric material in its fill. Spurrell quickly withdrew his identification of the site as a Neolithic flint mine.

Dunstable Downs, Bedfordshire
NGR: uncertain
NMR number: none assigned
Main published sources: Matthews 1963; 1989, 6; Horne 1996, 32
Comments: The site, originally suggested as a possible flint mine by Matthews (1963), was subsequently shown to be a gravel pit.

Drayton, Norfolk
NGR: TG 18881295, TG 18141460
NMR number: TG 11 SE 2, TG 11 SE 12
Comments: The site at TG 18881295 may represent exploitation of outcropping flint, although the area has seen recent extensive chalk quarrying. Nothing was seen at the other location that could indicate flint extraction.

East Horsley, Surrey
NGR: TQ 096516
NMR number: TQ 05 SE 5
Excavations: Todd 1949

Main published sources: Todd 1949; Wood 1952
Comments: Although there appears to have been a considerable quantity of Neolithic and later material on the surface, the shaft excavated by Todd was of medieval date at the earliest.

Easton, Norfolk
NGR: TG 147095
NMR number: TG 10 NW 2
Main published sources: Clarke 1912b; de Caux 1942
Comments: Recent quarrying has occurred in the area, and the lithic material recovered points to a number of different episodes of activity. There is nothing to indicate flint extraction.

Eaton, Norwich, Norfolk
NGR: TG 202063
NMR number: TG 20 NW 145
Main published sources: Greenwell 1870; Hawood 1912; 1919
Comments: Although reports of stray finds of flint implements and antlers are intriguing, the feature described by Hawood was clearly a solution pipe rather than a mine shaft.

Fairmile Bottom, Madehurst, West Sussex
NGR: SU 994099
NMR number: SU 90 NE 145
Comments: Flint flakes and a crude axe roughout have been recovered from an area showing surface evidence for quarrying. However, the location, at the foot of a steep scarp, is an unlikely one for flint mining, and chalk quarrying is a more likely explanation.

Fareham, Hampshire
NGR: SU 596069
NMR number: SU 50 NE 23
Excavations: South Hampshire Archaeological Rescue Group 1972
Main published sources: Hughes 1972; Fowler and Bennett 1972; Hughes and ApSimon 1977
Comments: An early interim statement raised the possibility of flint mining. However, lithic finds were predominantly Mesolithic and the features concerned were solution pipes.

Goodwood, Lavant, West Sussex
NGR: SU 876098
NMR number: SU 80 NE 22
Comments: Shallow pits reported by an Ordnance Survey field investigator probably represent 19th-century chalk and flint digging. There is no evidence to support a Neolithic date.

Great Down, Madehurst, West Sussex
NGR: SU 973113
NMR number: SU 91 SE 39

Comments: The location at the foot of a slope, coupled with a lack of lithic material suggests that the reported depressions are more likely to represent chalk quarrying than flint mining.

Great Massingham, Norfolk
NGR: TF 770221
NMR number: TF 72 SE 15
Main published sources: Plowright 1891
Comments: Field observation failed to find any traces of flint mining. The area has seen much carstone, gravel and chalk extraction. While the reported finds would not be unusual in a flint mine context, the account of their recovery during gravel extraction suggests that they did not come from a mine shaft.

Great Melton, Norfolk
NGR: TG 146087, TG 133075, TG 137066
NMR number: TG 10 NW 3
Main published sources: Clarke and Halls 1917
Comments: Access to the sites has not proved possible. Flint scatters and other stray finds are reported from the area, but numerous marl pits are known to exist in the vicinity.

Grimsditch Wood, Saffron Walden, Essex
NGR: TL 544407
NMR number: TL 54 SW 24
Main published sources: Morris 1924, 62–3
Comments: The hollows and depressions seem most likely to represent recent chalk pits. A few struck flints are present, but there is no evidence of flint mining debris.

Hackpen Hill, Winterbourne Monkton, Wiltshire
NGR: SU 121726
NMR number: SU 17 SW 147
Excavations: Kendall 1912
Main published sources: Kendall 1916; 1922
Comments: Although there is surface lithic evidence for prehistoric activity in the area, the pits examined by Kendall seem most likely to represent natural features or recent digging. There has been considerable post-medieval gravel and flint extraction in the area.

Hambledon Hill, Dorset
NGR: ST 849122
NMR number: ST 81 SW 68
Excavations: Mercer 1974–86
Main published sources: Mercer 1987
Comments: The published evidence is not conclusive. Medieval or later flint digging, for which there is considerable evidence on Hambledon Hill, seems a more plausible interpretation.

Highdown Hill, West Sussex
NGR: TQ 093044
NMR number: TQ 00 SE 150
Excavations: Irving 1860s; Lane Fox 1868
Main published sources: Irving 1857, 289–94; Lane Fox 1869a; 1869b; Engelen n.d.
Comments: None of the depressions are likely to represent flint mines. They are more likely to result from more recent activity, particularly chalk quarrying.

Lavant (Trumley Copse), West Sussex
NGR: SU 841089
NMR number: SU 80 NW 14
Comments: Shallow depressions apparently similar to the Lavant Caves site have been reported, although Ordnance Survey field investigation in 1971 found nothing of significance.

Lavant Caves, Lavant, West Sussex
NGR: SU 868099
NMR number: SU 80 NE 25
Excavations: Sussex Archaeological Society 1890s
Main published sources: Clinch 1905, 326–7; Allcroft 1916, 68–74
Comments: Surface evidence suggests chalk quarrying rather than flint mining. The underground workings – the caves – may be compared with chalk mines elsewhere in the country. Note also the involvement of Charles Dawson, a key figure in the Piltdown forgery controversy.

Liddington, Wiltshire
NGR: SU 215801
NMR number: SU 28 SW 96
Main published sources: Passmore 1940; 1943; Hirst and Rahtz 1996.
Comments: The depressions referred to by Passmore are more plausibly interpreted as the remains of late 19th-century flint quarrying. A pit or shaft encountered during excavations in 1976 was not examined to a sufficient extent to allow its date or function to be determined, although the evidence suggests a flint mine interpretation is unlikely.

Little Somborne, Hampshire
NGR: SU 393341, SU 395335
NMR number: SU 33 SE 24
Main published sources: Clay 1925b
Comments: Referred to by Clay as a 'flint factory site', and included in Engelen's (n.d.) list of flint mines. However, Clay's account makes it clear that only poor quality flint from on or just beneath the surface was being exploited.

Peppard Common, Rotherfield Peppard, Oxfordshire
NGR: SU 710814
NMR number: SU 78 SW 7
Excavations: Peake 1912; Smith 1913
Main published sources: Peake 1913; 1914; 1918
Comments: Ploughing and vegetation has obscured features examined by Peake on the lower slopes of a dry valley. Relatively recent surface quarries exist, in some cases having exploited the gravel above the chalk. Although Neolithic quarrying is possible, mining seems unlikely.

Pitstone Hill, Pitstone, Buckinghamshire
NGR: SP 949140
NMR number: SP 91 SW 21
Main published sources: Dyer and Hales 1961
Comments: This small group of quarries with irregular spoil heaps are more likely to result from medieval or later chalk extraction.

Riddlesdown, Greater London
NGR: TQ 325605 and area
NMR number: TQ 36 SW 20
Main published sources: Farley 1973, 28–9
Comments: Various earthworks have been noted on Riddlesdown, including the depressions tentatively identified as possible flint mine shafts. However, marl pits or other recent chalk extraction appear to be more plausible interpretations.

Ringland, Norfolk
NGR: TG 145123
NMR number: TG 11 SW 8
Excavations: W G Clarke 1914(?)
Main published sources: Clarke 1906; 1913; 1915a
Comments: Clarke's accounts suggest extraction from a shallow seam or outcrop rather than mining.

Salthouse, Norfolk
NGR: TG 078414
NMR number: TG 04 SE 49
Comments: The site is off the chalk. This fact, coupled with the recovery of ground flint axes and a lack of mining debris suggests that this was not an extraction site.

Stanhoe, Norfolk
NGR: TF 797379
NMR number: TF 73 NE 16
Main published sources: Anon 1978, 23
Comments: A concentration of struck flint has been noted and described as a 'suggested axe factory site', but there are no surface indications of

mining. The chalk here is covered by drift deposits and flint seams are likely to be at some depth.

St Peter's, Isle of Thanet, Kent
NGR: TR 3868 (precise location uncertain)
NMR number: TR 36 NE 23
Excavations: Lane Fox 1868
Main published sources: Lane Fox 1869c; Greenwell 1870, 439
Comments: Initial identification as a flint mine was rejected by Lane Fox himself after returning to complete the excavation. The feature seems likely to have been a marl pit.

Walbury, Berkshire
NGR: SU 373615
NMR number: SU 36 SE 5
Comments: Ordnance Survey field investigation in 1971 raised the possibility that depressions within Walbury Camp hillfort might represent flint mines, but preferred to interpret them as the result of recent chalk quarrying. Recent inspection of the site also strongly favours the latter.

Wanborough, Surrey
NGR: SU 911483
NMR number: SU 84 NE 38
Main published sources: Oakley *et al* 1939, 131–2
Comments: The available information is brief and contradictory, but a Neolithic date seems unlikely, with no finds of that period being recorded.

Warlingham, Chelsham and Farleigh, Surrey
NGR: TQ 355591
NMR number: TQ 35 NE 9
Main published sources: Farley 1973
Comments: The description of an underground chamber and tunnel suggests that a denehole is a more plausible interpretation. No Neolithic finds were reported.

Weybourne, Norfolk
NGR: TG 118415
NMR number: TG 14 SW 15
Excavations: Spurrell *c* 1883
Main published sources: Harrod 1852; Spurrell 1883
Comments: There is no evidence in favour of flint extraction. The pits are most likely to represent quarrying for ironstone.

Whipsnade Zoo, Bedfordshire
NGR: TL 002178
NMR number: TL 01 NW 27
Main published sources: Holgate 1991, 10
Comments: A series of depressions within

flamingo, wallaby, bear and cheetah pennings most likely to represent the quarrying of clay.

Windover Hill, Arlington, East Sussex

NGR: TQ 545034, TQ 541034
NMR number: TQ 50 SW 76, TQ 50 SW 77
Excavations: Holden 1971
Main published sources: Curwen 1928; Holden 1974
Comments: The quarrying would appear to be entirely medieval and later extraction of chalk and flint, primarily for building materials. Holden's limited excavation recovered nothing to support a Neolithic date.

Woodmansterne, Banstead, Surrey

NGR: TQ 2760 (precise location uncertain)

NMR number: TQ 26 SE 53
Main published sources: Johnston and Wright 1903, 152
Comments: A vague report of surface scatters in an area containing a few shallow pits. No clear link between the two was demonstrated, and there is no evidence that the pits represent Neolithic mine shafts.

Wye, Kent

NGR: TR 073466
NMR number: TR 04 NE 14
Excavations: Jenkins 1955
Main published sources: Petrie 1880, 9
Comments: Spoil from some pits overlies lynchets. Little struck flint is evident. Ironstone extraction is a more likely explanation than flint mining.

Appendix 2
Radiocarbon dates from flint mines

1. Radiocarbon dates from English flint mines obtained prior to the present survey

For Grime's Graves, *see* the full date list published by Ambers (1996); for others *see* Burleigh nd.
Dates below are quoted as uncalibrated years before present (ie 1950), with calibrated ranges in calendar years BC at 95% probability, calculated using the maximum intercept method of Stuiver and Reimer (1986) and calibration data from Pearson *et al* (1986).

Blackpatch, West Sussex

BM-290	5090±150 BP	4310 to 3530 Cal BC
		Antler pick excavated by J Pull from a gallery belonging to Shaft 4

Church Hill, West Sussex

BM-181	5340±150 BP	4490 to 3810 Cal BC
		Antler picks from gallery excavated by J Pull

Cissbury, West Sussex

BM-183	4720±150 BP	3900 to 3030 Cal BC
		Antler picks from a gallery
BM-184	4650±150 BP	3780 to 2920 Cal BC
		Antler picks from a gallery
BM-185	4730±150 BP	3910 to 3040 Cal BC
		Antler picks from shaft 6 (gallery ?)

NB material excavated by both Pull and Park Harrison has been radiocarbon dated.

Easton Down, Wiltshire

BM-190	4480±150 BP	3630 to 2700 Cal BC
		Antler picks from a gallery excavated by J F S Stone 1930–4

Harrow Hill, West Sussex

BM-182	4930±150 BP	4040 to 3370 Cal BC
		Antler pick from gallery excavated by Curwen 1924–5
BM-2071R	4900±120 BP	3990 to 3370 Cal BC
		Antler from basal fill of shaft 13, excavated by Sieveking 1982
BM-2075R	5020±110 BP	4040 to 3540 Cal BC
		Charcoal from basal fill of shaft 13, excavated by Sieveking 1982
BM-2097R	5140±110 BP	4240 to 3700 Cal BC
		Charcoal from shaft 13 fill, excavated by Sieveking 1982
BM-2098R	5350±150 BP	4500 to 3810 Cal BC
		Charcoal from shaft 13 fill, excavated by Sieveking 1982
BM-2099R	5040±120 BP	4220 to 3540 Cal BC
		Antler from basal fill of shaft 13, excavated by Sieveking 1982
BM-2124R	5060±90 BP	4040 to 3690 Cal BC
		Charcoal from fill of shaft 13, excavated by Sieveking 1982

Long Down, West Sussex

Ox-A1151	4900±100 BP	4000 to 3350 Cal BC
		Antler pick from fill of shaft excavated by Holgate 1984
OxA-1152	5050±100 BP	4250 to 3600 Cal BC
		Ox scapula from fill of shaft excavated by Holgate 1984

2. Radiocarbon dates obtained during this survey

The following dates were provided by the British Museum's Department of Scientific Research. Dates are quoted as uncalibrated years before present (1950), with calibrated ranges in calendar years BC at 95% probability, calculated using data from Pearson *et al* (1986) and the OxCal v2.18 calibration program.

Cissbury, West Sussex

BM-3082	5100±60 BP	4040 to 3780 Cal BC
		Antler from gallery at base of shaft
BM-3086	4710±60 BP	3640 to 3360 Cal BC
		Antler from base of shaft 27

Harrow Hill, West Sussex

BM-3084	4880±30 BP	3780 to 3740 Cal BC or
		3710 to 3630 Cal BC or
		3570 to 3540 Cal BC
		Antler from gallery 2, shaft 21
BM-3085	5070±50 BP	3990 to 3780 Cal BC
		Antler from the base of shaft 25

Martin's Clump, Hampshire

BM-3083	5150±70 BP	4230 to 4190 Cal BC or
		4150 to 3780 Cal BC
		Antler from base of shaft 2

List of references

Aldsworth, F G 1979 'A possible Neolithic oval barrow on Nore Down, West Marden'. *Sussex Archaeol Collect* **117**, 251

Aldsworth, F G 1983 'Prehistoric flint mines on Nore Down, West Marden'. *Sussex Archaeol Collect* **121**, 187–90

Allcroft, A H 1916 'Some earthworks of West Sussex'. *Sussex Archaeol Collect* **58**, 65–90

Ambers, J 1996 'Radiocarbon analyses from the Grime's Graves mines', *in* Longworth, I and Varndell, G (eds) *Excavations at Grimes Graves, Norfolk 1972–1976, Fasc 5: Mining in the Deeper Mines*. London: British Museum Press

Anon, 1902 [notes on discoveries at High Wycombe]. *Antiquary* **38**, 323

Anon, 1978 'A select list of archaeological discoveries for 1977: Norfolk'. *Counc Brit Archaeol Group 6 Bull* **24**, 20–4

Armstrong, A L 1921 'Flint-crust engravings, and associated implements from Grime's Graves, Norfolk'. *Proc Prehist Soc East Anglia* **3** (3), 434–43

Armstrong, A L 1927 'The Grime's Graves problem in the light of recent research'. *Proc Prehist Soc East Anglia* **5**, 91–136

Armstrong, A L 1934a 'The Percy Sladen Trust excavations, Grime's Graves, Norfolk'. Interim report 1927–1932. *Proc Prehist Soc East Anglia* **7** (1932–4), 57–61

Armstrong, A L 1934b 'Grime's Graves, Norfolk: report on the excavation of Pit 12'. *Proc Prehist Soc East Anglia* **7** (1932–4), 382–94

Atkin, M 1983 'The chalk tunnels of Norwich'. *Norfolk Archaeol* **38**, 313–20

Atkinson, R, Piggott, C M and Sanders, N 1951 *Excavations at Dorchester, Oxon*. Oxford: Ashmolean Museum

Ayers, B S 1990 'Building a fine city: the provision of flint, mortar and freestone in medieval Norwich', *in* Parsons, D (ed), *Stone: Quarrying and Building in England AD 43–1525*. Chichester: Phillimore, 217–27

Barne, J H, Robson, C F, Kaznowska, S S, Doody, J P, Davidson, N C, and Buck, A L 1995 *Coasts and Seas of the United Kingdom, Region 6, Eastern England: Flamborough Head to Great Yarmouth*. Peterborough: Joint Nature Conservation Committee

Barne, J H, Robson, C F, Kaznowska, S S, Doody, J P, Davidson, N C, and Buck, A L 1996a *Coasts and Seas of the United Kingdom, Region 10, South-West England: Seaton to the Roseland Peninsula*. Peterborough: Joint Nature Conservation Committee

Barne, J H, Robson, C F, Kaznowska, S S, Doody, J P, Davidson, N C, and Buck, A L 1996b *Coasts and Seas of the United Kingdom, Region 11, The Western Approaches: Falmouth Bay to Keifig*. Peterborough: Joint Nature Conservation Committee

Barnes, I, Boismer, W A, Cleal, R M J, Fitzpatrick, A P, and Roberts, M A 1995 *Early Settlement in Berkshire* (Wessex Archaeological Reports, **6**). Salisbury: Wessex Archaeology and the Oxford Archaeological Unit

Barrett J C, Bradley R, and Green M 1991 *Landscape, Monuments and Society*. Cambridge: Cambridge University Press

Barton, R N E 1992 *Hengistbury Head, Dorset, Vol 2: The Late Upper Palaeolithic and Early Mesolithic sites* (Oxford Univ Comm Archaeol, Monograph **34**). Oxford: Oxford Univ Comm Archaeol

Berridge, P 1985 'Mesolithic sites in the Yarty Valley'. *Proc Devon Archaeol Soc* **43**, 1–22

Berridge, P 1994 'Cornish axe factories: fact or fiction?', *in* Ashton, N, and David, A (eds), *Stories in Stone* (Lithic Stud Soc Occ Pap **4**). London: Lithic Stud Soc, 45–56

Betterman, P and Ackermand, D nd 'Comparison (of) flint (and) chert based on chemical data (and resulting in a nomenclatoric proposal)'. *Second International Symposium on Flint, May 1975, Maastricht*. Nederlandse Geologische Verenigin, 27

Betterman, P, Lein, R and Bush, P nd 'Geochemical investigations to genesis of flint in (the) Santonian limestone formations from Lagerdorf, SW Holstein, Germany'. *Second International Symposium on Flint, May 1975, Maastricht*. Nederlandse Geologische Verenigin, 26–7

Bird, J 1963 *The Major Seaports of the United Kingdom*. London: Hutchinson

Blagg, T F C 1990 'Building stone in Roman Britain', *in* Parsons, D (ed) *Stone: Quarrying and Building in England AD 43–1525*. Chichester: Phillimore, 33–50

Blomefield, Rev F 1739 *An Essay Towards a Topographical History of the County of Norfolk*. London: W Miller

Booth, A St J, and Stone J F S 1952 'A trial flint mine at Durrington, Wilts'. *Wiltshire Archaeol Natur Hist Mag* **54**, 381–8

Borkowski, W 1995a *Krzemionki Mining Complex: Deposit Management System*. Warsaw: Państwowe Muzeum Archeologiczne

Borkowski, W 1995b 'Prehistoric flint mines complex in

Krzemionki (Kielce Province)'. *Archaeologia Polona* **33**, 506–24

Borkowski, W 1997 'Deposit management system of the Krzemionki exploitation field', *in* Schild, R and Sulgostowska, Z (eds) *Man and Flint*. Warsaw: Institute of Archaeology and Ethnology, Polish Academy of Sciences, 41–8

Borkowski, W and Budziszewski, J 1995 'The use of striped flint in prehistory'. *Archaeologia Polona* **33**, 71–88

Borkowski, W, Migal, W, Salaciński, S and Zalewski, M 1995 'P L 20 Rybniki, Białystok Province'. *Archaeologia Polona* **33**, 524–31

Bostyn, F and Lanchon, Y (eds) 1992 *Jablines le Haut-Château (Seine-et-Marne): une minière de silex au Néolithique* (Documents d'Archéologie Française, 35). Paris: Editions de la Maison des Sciences de l'Homme

Bostyn, F and Lanchon, Y (eds) 1995 'The Neolithic flint-mine at Jablines, "le Haut-Chateau" (Seine-et-Marne)'. *Archaeologia Pologna* **33**, 297–310

Bowden, M 1991 *Pitt Rivers: the Life and Archaeological Work of Lieutenant-General Augustus Henry Lane Fox Pitt Rivers, DCL, FRS, FSA*. Cambridge: Cambridge University Press

Bradley, R 1989 'Herbert Toms – a pioneer of analytical field survey', *in* Bowden, M, Mackay D, and Topping, P (eds) *From Cornwall to Caithness. Some aspects of British Field Archaeology. Papers presented to Norman V Quinnell* (Brit Archaeol Rep, British Series **209**). Oxford: Brit Archaeol Rep, 29–47

Bradley, R 1993 *Altering the Earth* (Soc Antiq Scotland Monograph Series, **8**). Edinburgh: Soc Antiq Scotland

Bradley, R and Chambers, R 1988 'A new study of the cursus complex at Dorchester on Thames'. *Oxford J Archaeol* **7**, 271–89

Bradley, R and Edmonds, M 1993 *Interpreting the Axe Trade*. Cambridge: Cambridge University Press

Briart, A, Cornet, F and de Lehaie, A H 1868 'Rapport sur les découvertes géologiques et archéologiques faites à Spiennes en 1867'. *Mémoires … de la Société des Sciences, des Arts … du Hainaut, année 1866-7*. Mons

Briggs, C S 1976 'Notes on the distribution of some raw materials in later prehistoric Britain', *in* Burgess, C and Miket, R (eds) *Settlement and Economy in the Third and Second Millennia BC* (Brit Archaeol Rep, British Series **33**). Oxford: Brit Archaeol Rep, 267–82

Briggs, C S 1989 'Axe-making traditions in Cumbrian Stone'. *Archaeol J* **146**, 1–43

Bristow, R, Mortimore, R, and Wood, C, 1997 'Lithostratigraphy for mapping the Chalk of southern England'. *Proc Geol Ass* **108**, 293–315

Brooks, I P 1989 'Debugging the system: the characterization of flint by micropalaeontology', *in* Brooks, I and Phillips, P (eds) *Breaking the Stony Silence: Papers from the Sheffield Lithics Conference 1988* (Brit Archaeol Rep, British Series **213**). Oxford: Brit Archaeol Rep, 53–74

Bruce-Mitford, R L S 1938 'A hoard of Neolithic axes from Peaslake, Surrey'. *Antiq J* **18**, 279–84

Bruce-Mitford, R L S 1952 'A late-medieval chalk mine at Thetford'. *Norfolk Archaeol* **30**, 220–2

Burleigh, R nd 'Radiocarbon dates for flint mines', *in* Engelen, F H G (ed) *Second International Symposium on Flint, May 1975, Maastricht*. Nederlandse Geologische Verenigin, 89–91

Burleigh, R, Clutton-Brock J, Felder P J and Sieveking G de G 1977 'A further consideration of Neolithic dogs with special reference to a skeleton from Grime's Graves (Norfolk), England'. *J Archaeol Sci* **4**, 353–66

Bush, P R nd 'The use of trace elements in the archaeological classification of cherts', *in* Engelen, F H G (ed) *Second International Symposium on Flint, May 1975, Maastrict*. Nederlandse Geologische Verenigin, 47–8

Bush, P R and Sieveking, G de G 1986 'Geochemistry and the provenance of flint axes', *in* Sieveking, G de G and Hart, M B (eds) *The Scientific Study of Flint and Chert*. Cambridge: Cambridge University Press, 133–40

Buurman, P nd 'Biogenic and inorganic cherts', *in* Engelen, F H G (ed) *Second International Symposium on Flint, May 1975, Maastricht*. Nederlandse Geologische Verenigin, 23–5

Care, V 1979 'The production and distribution of Mesolithic axes in Southern England'. *Proc Prehist Soc* **45**, 93–102

Castle, S 1971 'Archaeological survey of South West Hertfordshire' *Watford South West Hertfordshire Archaeol Soc* (14 October, 1971), 1–11

Catt, J A 1986 'The nature, origin and geomorphological significance of Clay-with-flints', *in* Sieveking, G de G and Hart, M B (eds) *The Scientific Study of Flint and Chert*. Cambridge: Cambridge University Press, 151–60

Clark, J G D and Piggott, S 1933 'The age of the British flint mines'. *Antiquity* **7**, 166–83

Clarke, R R 1935 'Notes on the archaeology of Markshall'. *Norfolk Archaeol* **25**, 354–67

Clarke, W G 1906 'A "Cissbury Type" station at Ringland'. *Trans Norfolk Norwich Naturalists Soc* **8**, 224–8

Clarke, W G 1908 'A Neolithic flint quarry'. *Proc Prehist Soc East Anglia* **1**, 116

Clarke, W G 1912a 'Implements of Sub-Crag Man in Norfolk'. *Proc Prehist Soc East Anglia* **1**, 160–8

Clarke, W G 1912b 'Cissbury type implements at Easton'. *Proc Prehist Soc East Anglia* **1**, 240–1

Clarke, W G 1913 'Norfolk implements of Palaeolithic "Cave" types'. *Proc Prehist Soc East Anglia* **1**, 340–1

Clarke, W G 1915a 'A prehistoric flint-pit at Ringland'. *Proc Prehist Soc East Anglia* **2**, 148–51

Clarke, W G (ed) 1915b *Report on the Excavations at Grime's Graves, Weeting, Norfolk, March–May 1914*. London: Prehistoric Society of East Anglia

Clarke, W G and Halls, H H 1917 'A "Cissbury Type" station at Great Melton'. *Proc Prehist Soc East Anglia* **2**, 374–80

Clason, A T 1981 'The flintminer as a farmer, hunter, and antler collector'. *Third International Symposium on Flint, 24–27 May 1979, Maastricht*. Nederlandse Geologische Verenigin, 119–25

Clay, R C C, 1925a 'A gunflint factory site in south Wilts'. *Antiq J* **5**, 423–6

Clay, R C C 1925b 'A flint factory site at Little Somborne, Hants'. *Proc Prehist Soc East Anglia* **5**, 67–72

Clayton, C J 1986 'The chemical environment of flint

formation in Upper Cretaceous Chalk', *in* Sieveking, G de G and Hart, M B (eds), *The Scientific Study of Flint and Chert*. Cambridge: Cambridge University Press, 43–54

Clinch, G 1905 'Early Man'. *The Victoria History of the County of Sussex*, Vol I. London: Constable, 309–32

Clough, T H McK and Cummins, W A (eds) 1988 *Stone Axe Studies Volume 2: the Petrology of Prehistoric Stone Implements from the British Isles* (Counc Brit Archaeol Res Rep **67**). London: Counc Brit Archaeol

Clough, T H McK and Green B 1972 'The petrological identification of stone implements from East Anglia'. *Proc Prehist Soc* **38**, 108–55

Clutton-Brock, J 1984 *Excavations at Grimes Graves, Norfolk 1972-1976*, Fasc 1: *Neolithic Antler Picks from Grimes Graves, Norfolk and Durrington Walls, Wiltshire: A Biometrical Analysis*. London: British Museum Press

Coles J M, Hibbert, F A, and Orme, B J 1973 'Prehistoric roads and tracks in Somerset, England: 3. The Sweet Track'. *Proc Prehist Soc* **39**, 256–93

Craddock, P T, Cowell, M R, Leese, M N, Hughes, M J 1983 'The trace element composition of polished flint axes as an indicator of source'. *Archaeometry* **25**, 135–63

Cunliffe, B 1973 'Chalton, Hants: the evolution of a landscape'. *Antiq J* **53**, 173–90

Curwen, E C 1928 'The antiquities of Windover Hill' *Sussex Archaeol Collect* **69**, 92–101

Curwen, E C 1929 'Excavations in the Trundle, Goodwood, 1928'. *Sussex Archaeol Collect* **70**, 32–85

Curwen, E C 1930 Wolstonbury. *Sussex Archaeol Collect* **71**, 237–45

Curwen, E C 1936 'Excavations in Whitehawk Camp, Brighton, third season, 1935'. *Sussex Archaeol Collect* **77**, 60–92

Curwen, E and Curwen, E C 1922 'Notes on the archaeology of Burpham and the neighbouring Downs'. *Sussex Archaeol Collect* **63**, 1–53

Curwen, E and Curwen, E C 1926 'Harrow Hill flint-mine excavation 1924–5'. *Sussex Archaeol Collect* **67**, 103–38

Curwen, E and Curwen, E C 1927 'Probable flint mines near Tolmere Pond, Findon'. *Sussex Notes and Queries* **1** (May 1927), 168–70 and 246–7

Curwen, E C and Ross-Williamson, R P 1931 'The date of Cissbury camp'. *Antiq J* **11**, 13–36

Darvill, T 1996 'Neolithic buildings in England, Wales and the Isle of Man', *in* Darvill, T and Thomas, J (eds) *Neolithic Houses in Northwest Europe and Beyond* (Oxbow Monograph **57**). Oxford: Oxbow, 77–112

de Caux, H 1942 'A prehistoric site in the Yare valley'. *Norfolk Archaeol* **28**, 71–5

Di Lernia, S, Fiorentino, G, Galiberti, A, and Basili, R 1995 'The Early Neolithic mine of Defensola 'A' (I18): flint exploitation in the Gargano area'. *Archaeologia Polona* **33**, 119–32

Down, A 1993 *Chichester Excavations 8*. Chichester: Chichester District Council

Drewett, P L 1977 'Neolithic and Bronze Age settlements and their territories', *in* Drewett, P L *et al* 'Rescue archaeology in Sussex, 1976,' *Bull Inst Archaeol* **14**, 15–25

Drewett, P L 1978 'Neolithic Sussex', *in* Drewett, P L (ed) *The Archaeology of Sussex to AD 1500* (Counc Brit Archaeol Res Rep **29**). London: Counc Brit Archaeol, 23–9

Drewett, P L 1983a. 'A Peterborough Ware sherd from the Long Down flint mines'. *Sussex Archaeological Collections* **121**, 95

Drewett, P L 1983b. 'An early 3rd millennium sherd from the Long Down Flint Mines, West Sussex'. *Sussex Archaeological Collections* **121**, 194–5

Durden, T 1995 'The production of specialised flintwork in the later Neolithic: a case study from the Yorkshire Wolds'. *Proc Prehist Soc* **61**, 409–32

Durden, T 1996 'Lithics in the north of England: production and consumption on the Yorkshire Wolds', *in* Frodsham, P (ed) 'Neolithic studies in no-man's land: papers on the Neolithic of Northern England from the Trent to the Tweed', *Northern Archaeol* **13/14**, 79–86

Dyer, J F, and Hales, A J 1961. 'Pitstone Hill: a study in field archaeology'. *Rec Buckinghamshire* **17** (1), 49–56

Edmonds, E A, McKeown, M C and Williams, M 1975 *South-West England* (British Regional Geologies). London: HMSO

Edmonds, M 1995 *Stone Tools and Society*. London: Batsford

Edmonds, M, Sheridan, A, and Tipping, R 1992 'Survey and excavation at Creag na Caillich, Killin, Perthshire'. *Proc Soc Antiq Scotland* **122**, 77–112

Ellaby, R, 1987 'Upper Palaeolithic and Mesolithic', *in* Bird, J, and Bird, D G (eds) *The Archaeology of Surrey to 1540*. Guildford: Surrey Archaeological Society, 53–70

Ellis, C 1986 'The postglacial molluscan succession of the South Downs dry valley', *in* Sieveking, G de G and Hart, M B (eds) *The Scientific Study of Flint and Chert*. Cambridge: Cambridge University Press, 175–84

Engelen, F H (nd) 'Prehistorische (vuur) steenwinning in Europa', *in* Engelen, F H (ed), *Second International Symposium on Flint, May 1975, Maastricht*. Staringia **3**, 92–4

Evans, J G, Jones, H and Keepax, C 1981 'Subfossil land-snail faunas from Grimes Graves and other Neolithic flint mines', *in* Mercer, R J *Grimes Graves, Norfolk: Excavations 1971–72, Volume 1* (Dept of Environment Archaeol Rep **11**). London: HMSO, 104–11

Farley, M 1973 *Guide to the Local Antiquities*. Surrey: Bourne Society

Fasham, P J 1979 'The excavation of a triple barrow in Micheldever Wood, Hampshire'. *Proc Hampshire Fld Club Archaeol Soc* **35**, 5–40

Felder, P J 1981 'Prehistoric flint mining at Rijckholt-St. Geertruid (Netherlands) and Grimes Graves (England)', *in* Engelen F H G (ed) *Third International Symposium on Flint, 24–27 May 1979, Maastricht*. Staringa **6**, 57–62

Field, D 1982 'A miniature flint axe from Cissbury'. *Sussex Archaeol Collect* **120**, 205–7

Field, D 1989 'Tranchet axes and Thames Picks: Mesolithic core-tools from the west London Thames'. *Trans London Middlesex Archaeol Soc* **40**, 1–26

Field, D, Nicolaysen, P, Waters, K, Winser, K and
    Ketteringham, L L 1991 'Prehistoric material from
    Slines Oaks and Worms Heath, Chelsham'. *Surrey
    Archaeol Collect* **80**, 133–46
Figg, W, 1853 '... Objects exhibited ...'. *Archaeol J* **10**, 259
Fisher, C 1982 'Early chalk tramways at Whitlingham'.
    J Norfolk Industrial Archaeol Soc **3** (2), 89–91
Fisher, P F 1991 'The physical environment of Cranborne
    Chase', *in* Barrett, J, Bradley, R and Hall, M (eds),
    Papers on the Prehistoric Archaeology of Cranborne Chase
    (Oxbow Monograph **11**). Oxford: Oxbow, 11–19
Flood, J 1983 *The Archaeology of the Dreamtime*. London: Collins
Forrest, A J 1983 *Masters of Flint*. Suffolk: Lavenham Press
Fowler, M J F 1987 'Over Wallop – Martin's Clump'. *Archaeology
    and Historic Buildings in Hampshire: Annual Report for 1986*.
    Winchester: Hampshire County Council Planning Dept **4**
Fowler, M J F 1992. 'A gunflint industry at Martin's Clump,
    Over Wallop, Hampshire'. *Proc Hampshire Fld Club
    Archaeol Soc* **48**, 135–42
Fowler, P J and Bennett, J 1972 'M5 and Archaeology'. (*Counc
    Brit Archaeol Groups XII and XIII) Archaeol Rev* **7**, 5–10

Gabel, W C 1957 'The Campignian Tradition and European
    flint mining'. *Antiquity* **31**, 90–2
Gardiner, J P 1984 'Lithic distributions and Neolithic
    settlement patterns in Central Southern England', *in*
    Bradley R and Gardiner J P (eds) *Neolithic Studies: a
    Review of Some Research* (Brit Archaeol Rep, British Series
    133). Oxford: Brit Archaeol Rep, 15–40
Gardiner, J P 1987 'Tales of the unexpected: approaches to
    the assessment and interpretation of museum flint
    collections', *in* Brown, A G and Edmonds, M R (eds)
    Lithic Analysis and Later Prehistory (Brit Archaeol Rep,
    British Series **162**). Oxford: Brit Archaeol Rep, 49–63
Gardiner, J P 1990 'Flint procurement and Neolithic axe
    production on the South Downs: a re-assessment'.
    Oxford J Archaeol **9**:2 (July 1990), 119–40.
Gaster, C T A 1944 'The stratigraphy of the chalk of Sussex:
    Part 3, Western area – Arun gap to the Hampshire
    boundary'. *Proc Geol Ass* **55**, 173–88.
Gibbard, P L 1986 'Flint gravels in the Quaternary of
    southern England', *in* Sieveking, G de G and Hart M B,
    (eds) *The Scientific Study of Flint and Chert*. Cambridge:
    Cambridge University Press, 141–9
Goodman, C H, Frost, M, Curwen, E and Curwen, E C 1924
    'Blackpatch flint mine excavations, 1922: report
    prepared on behalf of the Worthing Archaeological
    Society'. *Sussex Archaeol Collect* **65**, 69–111
Gould, R 1977 'Ethno-archaeology: or, where do models
    come from?', *in* Wright, R S V (ed) *Stone Tools as
    Cultural Markers*. New Jersey: Humanities Press
Greenwell, W 1870 'On the opening of Grime's Graves in
    Norfolk'. *J Ethnol Soc London*, New Series **2**, 419–39
Griffith, A F 1924 'Notes and queries'. *Sussex Archaeol Collect*
    65, 260
Grimes, W F 1979 'The history of implement petrology in
    Britain', *in* Clough, T H McK and Cummins, W A (eds)
    Stone Axe Studies (Counc Brit Archaeol Res Rep **23**).
    London: Counc Brit Archaeol, 5–12

Guirr, H, Phillips, P, and May, J 1989 'Flintwork from
    Neolithic structures and contexts at Dragonby, South
    Humberside', *in* Brooks, I and Phillips, P (eds) *Breaking
    the Stony Silence: Papers from the Sheffield Lithics Conference
    1988* (Brit Archaeol Rep, British Series **213**). Oxford:
    Brit Archaeol Rep, 109–30

Halls, H H 1908. (untitled note on flint axes from Whitling-
    ham). *Proc Prehist Soc East Anglia* **1**, 111 and plate XVI
Halls, H H 1914 'Implements from a station at Cranwich,
    Norfolk'. *Proc Prehist Soc East Anglia* **1**, 454–7
Hamilton, B C 1933. 'Suspected flint mines on Bow Hill'.
    Sussex Notes and Queries **4** (8) (November 1933), 246–7
Harris, A P 1990 'Building stone in Norfolk', *in* Parsons, D
    (ed) *Stone: Quarrying and Building in England* AD
    43–1525. Chichester: Phillimore, 207–16
Harrison, D J 1990 'Marine aggregate survey Phase 3: East
    Coast'. *British Geological Survey, Marine Report*
    WB/90/17. Nottingham: British Geological Survey
Harrison, J P 1877a 'On marks found upon chalk at
    Cissbury'. *J Anthropol Inst* **6**, 263–71
Harrison, J P 1877b 'Report on some further discoveries at
    Cissbury'. *J Anthropol Inst* **6**, 430–2
Harrison, J P 1878 'Additional discoveries at Cissbury'.
    J Anthropol Inst **7**, 412–33
Harrod, H 1852 'On the Weybourne Pits'. *Norfolk Archaeol* **3**,
    232–40
Hartridge, R 1978 'Excavations at the prehistoric and
    Romano-British site on Slonk Hill, Shoreham, Sussex'.
    Sussex Archaeol Collect **116**, 69–141
Hawood, F N 1912 'The chipping of flints by natural
    agencies'. *Proc Prehist Soc East Anglia* **2**, 185–93
Hawood, F N 1919 'The origin of the "Rostro-Carinate
    Implements" and other chipped flints from the
    Basement Beds of East Anglia'. *Proc Prehist Soc East
    Anglia* **3**, 118–46
Head, J F 1955 *Early Man in South Buckinghamshire*. Bristol:
    John Wright and Sons
Healy, F 1991 'The hunting of the floorstone', *in* Schofield, A
    J (ed) *Interpreting Artefact Scatters; Contributions to
    Ploughzone Archaeology* (Oxbow Monograph **4**). Oxford:
    Oxbow, 29–37
Henson, D 1985 'The flint resources of Yorkshire and the East
    Midlands'. *Lithics* **6**, 2–9
Henson, D 1989 'Away from the core? A northerner's view of
    flint exploitation', *in* Brooks, I and Phillips, P (eds)
    *Breaking the Stony Silence: Papers from the Sheffield Lithics
    Conference 1988* (Brit Archaeol Rep, British Series **213**).
    Oxford: Brit Archaeol Rep, 5–32
Hewitt, H D 1935. 'Further notes on the Chalk of the
    Thetford District'. *Proc Geol Ass* **46**, 18–37
Hillam J, Groves, C M, Brown, D M, Baillie, M G L, Coles, J M
    and Coles, B J 1990 'Dendrochronology of the English
    Neolithic'. *Antiquity* **64** (243), 210–20
Hirst, S, and Rahtz, P 1996 'Liddington Castle and the Battle
    of Badon: excavations and research 1976'. *Archaeol J*
    153, 1–59
Hoare, R C 1810 *The History of Ancient Wiltshire*. London:
    William Miller

Holden, E W 1974 'Flint mines on Windover Hill, Wilmington'. *Sussex Archaeol Collect* **112**, 154

Holgate, R 1985 'Neolithic excavations in Sussex, Summer 1985'. *Sussex Archaeol Soc Newsletter* **47** (December 1985), 455

Holgate, R 1988 'Further investigations at the later Neolithic domestic site and Napoleonic "camp" at Bullock Down, near Eastbourne, East Sussex'. *Sussex Archaeol Collect* **126**, 21–30

Holgate, R 1989 *The Neolithic Flint Mines in Sussex: a Plough Damage Assessment and Site Management Report*. London: Field Archaeology Unit, Institute of Archaeology

Holgate, R 1991 *Prehistoric Flint Mines*. Princes Risborough: Shire Publications

Holgate, R 1995a 'Neolithic flint mining in Britain'. *Archaeologia Polona* **33**, 133–61

Holgate, R 1995b 'GB4 Harrow Hill near Findon, West Sussex'. *Archaeologia Polona* **33**, 347–50

Holgate, R 1995c 'GB6 Long Down near Chichester, West Sussex'. *Archaeologia Polona* **33**, 350–2

Holgate, R and Butler, C forthcoming 'The Neolithic flint mines in Sussex: results of recent fieldwork'. *Sussex Archaeol Collect*

Holland, J D 1994 'English flint on the coast of Maine'. *Chips* **6** (2), 4

Holleyman, G 1937 'Harrow Hill Excavations, 1936'. *Sussex Archaeol Collect* **78**, 230–52

Horne, B 1996 'Will the real Neolithic please stand up?' *J Manshead Archaeol Soc* **36** (August 1996), 22–39

Hughes, M F 1972 'Summary report on rescue excavations on M27 motorway route — Portsdown'. *South Hampshire Archaeological Rescue Group Newsletter*, **6** (August 1972), 8–10

Hughes, M F and ApSimon, A M 1977 'A Mesolithic flint working site on the south coast motorway (M27) near Fort Wallington, Fareham, Hampshire 1972'. *Proc Hampshire Fld Club Archaeol Soc* **34**, 23–36

Irving, G V 1857 'On the camps at Cissbury, Sussex'. *J Brit Archaeol Ass* **13**, 274–94

Jarvis, I and Woodroof, P B 1984 'Stratigraphy of the Cenomanian and basal Turonian (Upper Cretaceous) between Branscombe and Seaton, S E Devon, England'. *Proc Geol Ass* **95**, 193–215

Johnson, S, 1976 *The Roman Forts of the Saxon Shore*. London: Elek

Johnston, W and Wright, W 1903 *Neolithic Man in North East Surrey*. London: Elliot Stock

Jones, E L, 1960 'Eighteenth-century changes in Hampshire chalkland farming'. *Agricultural Hist Rev* **8**, 5–19

Jonsson, L 1992 *Birds of Europe*. London: Christopher Helm

Jukes-Brown, A J 1900 *The Cretaceous Rocks of Britain*, Vol 1: *The Gault and Upper Greensand of England*. London: Memoirs of the Geological Survey of the UK

Jukes-Brown, A J 1903 *The Cretaceous Rocks of Britain*, Vol 2: *The Lower and Middle Chalk of England*. London: Memoirs of the Geological Survey of the UK

Kelly, G I 1994 'Underneath Norwich: chalk and flint workings'. *Annual Bull Norfolk Archaeol Hist Res Group* **3**, 12–16

Kendall, H G O 1916 'Excavations on Hackpen Hill, Wilts'. *Proc Soc Antiq London*, 2 Ser **28**, 26–48

Kendall, H G O 1922 'Scraper core industries in North Wilts'. *Proc Prehist Soc East Anglia* **3**, 515–41

Kendall, P F 1907 'Geology', *in* Page, W (ed) *The Victoria History of the County of Yorkshire*, Vol I. London: Constable, 1–98

Kendrick, T D and Hawkes, C F C 1932 *Archaeology in England and Wales 1914–1931*. London: Methuen and Co

Kitton, F 1878 'William Arderon, FRS, an old Norwich naturalist'. *Trans Norfolk Norwich Natur Soc* **2**, 429–59

Kraaijenhagen, F C 1981 'State of affairs at Rijckholt', *in* Engelen F H G (ed) *Third Symposium on Flint, 24–27 May 1979, Maastrict*. Staringia **6**, 7–8

Lane Fox, A H 1869a 'An examination into the character and probable origins of the hillforts of Sussex'. *Archaeologia* **42**, 27–52

Lane Fox, A H 1869b 'Further remarks on the hillforts of Sussex: being an account of the excavations of the hillforts at Cissbury and Highdown'. *Archaeologia* **42**, 53–76

Lane Fox, A H 1869c 'On some flint implements found associated with Roman remains in Oxfordshire and the Isle of Thanet'. *J Ethnol Soc London*, New Series **1**, 1–12

Lane Fox, A H 1876 'Excavations in Cissbury Camp, Sussex; being a report of the Exploration Committee of the Anthropological Institute for the year 1875'. *J Anthropol Inst Great Britain Ireland* **5**, 357–90

Law, W 1927 'Flint mines on Church Hill, Findon'. *Sussex Notes and Queries* **1** (7) (August 1927), 222–4.

Lawson, A J, Martin, E A and Priddy, D 1981 *The Barrows of East Anglia* (East Anglian Archeol Rep **12**). Norwich: Norfolk Archaeological Unit

Layard, N F 1922. 'Prehistoric cooking places in Norfolk. *Proc Prehist Soc East Anglia* **3**, 483–98

Legge, A J 1992. *Excavations at Grimes Graves, Norfolk 1972–1976, Fasc 4: Animals, Environment and the Bronze Age Economy*. London: British Museum Press

Longworth, I, Ellison, A and Rigby, V 1988 *Excavations at Grimes Graves, Norfolk 1972–1976*, Fasc 2: *The Neolithic, Bronze Age and Later Pottery*. London: British Museum Press

Longworth, I, Herne, A, Varndell, G and Needham, S 1991. *Excavations at Grimes Graves, Norfolk 1972–1976*. Fasc 3: *Bronze Age Flint, Chalk and Metal Working*. London: British Museum Press.

Longworth, I and Varndell, G 1996 *Excavations at Grimes Graves, Norfolk 1972–1976*, Fasc 5: *Mining in the Deeper Mines*. London: British Museum Press

Loveday, J 1962 'Plateau deposits on the Southern Chilterns'. *Proc Geol Ass* **73**, 83–102

Lowther, A W G 1943 'Bronze-Iron Age and Roman finds at Ashtead'. *Surrey Archaeol Collect* **41**, 93–8.

Lubbock, J 1865 *Pre-historic Times, as Illustrated by Ancient Remains, and the Manners and Customs of Modern Savages*.

London: Williams and Norgate

Lyell, C 1863 *The Geological Evidences of the Antiquity of Man, with Remarks on Theories of the Origin of the Species by Variation*. London: John Murray

McCann, T J 1997 'The Lavant Caves revisited'. *Sussex Archaeol Collect* **135**, 311

McNabb, J, Felder, P J, Kinnes, I and Sieveking, G 1996 'An archive on recent excavations at Harrow Hill, Sussex'. *Sussex Archaeol Collect* **134**, 21–37

Manby, T G 1979 'Typology, materials, and distribution of flint and stone axes in Yorkshire', *in* Clough, T H McK and Cummins, W A (eds) *Stone Axe Studies* (Counc Brit Archaeol Res Rep **23**). London: Counc Brit Archaeol, 65–81

Manby, T G 1988 'The Neolithic in Eastern Yorkshire', *in* Manby, T G (ed) *Archaeology in Eastern Yorkshire*. Sheffield: Department of Archaeology and Prehistory, University of Sheffield, 35–88.

Manning, C R 1855 'Note on Grime's Graves'. *Norfolk Archaeol* **4**, 356.

Manning, C R 1872 'Grime's Graves, Weeting'. *Norfolk Archaeol* **7**, 169–77.

Manning, W H, 1995 'Ritual or refuse: the Harrow Hill enclosure considered', *in* Raftery, B (ed) *Sites and Sights of the Iron Age* (Oxbow Monograph **56**). Oxford: Oxbow, 133–8

Mason, H J 1978 *Flint the Versatile Stone*. Ely: Providence Press.

Matthews, C L 1963 *Ancient Dunstable: a Prehistory of the District*. Dunstable: Manshead Archaeol Soc

Matthews, C L 1989 *Ancient Dunstable: a Prehistory of the District* (revised edition). Dunstable: Manshead Archaeol Soc

Matthiessen, P (ed) 1989. *George Catlin: North American Indians*. Harmondsworth: Penguin Books

Mercer, R 1981a. *Grimes Graves, Norfolk: Excavations 1971–2, Volume 1* (Dept of the Environment Archaeol Rep **11**). London: HMSO

Mercer, R 1981b. *Grimes Graves, Norfolk: Excavations 1971–2, Volume 2* (Dept of the Environment Archaeol Rep **11**). London: HMSO

Mercer, R 1987 'A flint quarry in the Hambledon Hill Neolithic enclosure complex', *in* Sieveking, G de G and Newcomer, M H (eds) *The Human Uses of Flint and Chert: Proceedings of the Fourth International Flint Symposium, held at Brighton Polytechnic 10–15 April 1983*. Cambridge: Cambridge University Press

Moore, C N 1979 'Stone axes from the East Midlands', *in* Clough, T H McK and Cummins, W A (eds) *Stone Axe Studies* (Counc Brit Archaeol Res Rep **23**). London: Counc Brit Archaeol, 82–6

Morris, G 1924 'Some Neolithic sites in the upper valley of the Essex Cam'. *Essex Naturalist* **20**, 49–68.

Mortimer, J R 1878 'On the flints of the chalk of Yorkshire'. *Proc Geol Ass* **5**, 344–54

Mortimer, J R 1905 *Forty Years Researches in British and Saxon Burial Mounds of East Yorkshire*. London: Brown

Mortimore, R N 1982 'The stratigraphy and sedimentation of the Turonian-Campanian in the Southern Province of England'. *Zitteliana* **10**, 27–41

Mortimore, R N 1986a 'Controls on Upper Cretaceous sedimentation in the South Downs, with particular reference to flint distribution', *in* Sieveking, G de G and Hart, M B (eds) *The Scientific Study of Flint and Chert*. Cambridge: Cambridge University Press, 21–42

Mortimore, R N 1986b 'Stratigraphy of the Upper Cretaceous White Chalk of Sussex'. *Proc Geol Ass* **97** (2), 97–139

Mortimore, R N and Wood, C J 1986 'The distribution of flint in the English Chalk, with particular reference to the "Brandon Flint Series" and the high Turonian flint maximum', *in* Sieveking, G de G and Hart, M B (eds) *The Scientific Study of Flint and Chert*. Cambridge: Cambridge University Press, 7–42

Needham, S 1996 'Chronology and periodisation in the British Bronze Age'. *Acta Archaeologia* **67**, 121–40

O'Brien, W 1995. 'Ross Island and the origins of Irish-British metallurgy', *in* Waddell, J, and Shee Twohig, E (eds) *Ireland in the Bronze Age: Proceedings of the Dublin Conference, April 1995*. Dublin: The Stationery Office, 38–48

Oakley, K 1902 'Ancient Flint Mine'. *Mus J* **2**, 156

Oakley, K P, Rankine, W F, Lowther, A W G 1939 *A Survey of the Prehistory of the Farnham District*. Guildford: Surrey Archaeological Society

Palmer, S 1970 'The stone-age industries of the Isle of Portland, Dorset and the utilization of Portland Chert as artefact material'. *Proc Prehist Soc* **36**, 82–115

Park Harrison, J 1877a 'On marks found upon Chalk at Cissbury'. *J Anthropol Inst* **6**, 263–71

Park Harrison, J 1877b 'Report on some further discoveries at Cissbury'. *J Anthropol Inst* **6**, 430–42

Park Harrison, J 1878 'Additional discoveries at Cissbury'. *J Anthropol Inst* **7**, 412–33

Passmore, A D 1903 'Wiltshire Archaeological Notes'. Devizes Museum Archive, Mss.

Passmore, A D 1940 'Flint mines at Liddington Hill'. *Wiltshire Archaeol Mag* **49**, 118–19

Passmore, A D 1943 'A flint implement in a horned handle from near Liddington, Wiltshire'. *Antiq J* **23**, 52–3

Patterson, L W and Sollberger, J B 1979. 'Water treatment of flint'. *Lithic Technol* **8** (3: Dec 1979). University of Texas: Centre for Archaeological Research, 50–1

Peake, A E 1913. 'An account of a flint factory, with some new types of flints, excavated at Peppard Common, Oxon'. *Archaeol J* **70**, 33–68

Peake, A E 1914 'Notes on implements from the factory sites at Peppard, Oxon'. *Proc Prehist Soc East Anglia* **1** (4), 404–20

Peake, A E 1915 *Report on the Excavations at Grime's Graves, Weeting, Norfolk, March–May 1914*. London: Prehistoric Society of East Anglia

Peake, A E 1917 'Further excavations at Grimes Graves'. *Proc Prehist Soc East Anglia* **2** (3), 409–36

Peake, A E 1918 'Surface Palaeolithic implements from the Chilterns'. *Proc Prehsit Soc East Anglia* **2**, 578–87

Pearson, G W, Pilcher, J R, Baillie, M G L, Corbett, D M, and Qua, F 1986 'High-precision C14 measurement of Irish oaks to show the natural C14 variations from AD 1840–5210 BC'. *Radiocarbon* **28**, 911–34

Petrie, W M F 1880 'Notes on Kentish Earthworks'. *Archaeologia Cantiana* **13**, 8–16

Pettigrew, Rev S T 1853 'Note on Grime's Graves'. *J Brit Archaeol Ass* **8**, 77

Phillips, P 1986 'Raw material determination and analysis of lithic assemblages from excavations and surveys in Nottinghamshire and Lincolnshire, England', *in* Biro, K T (ed) *Papers for the 1st International Conference on Prehistoric Flint Mining and Lithic Raw Material Identification in the Carpathian Basin, Budapest, Sumeg.* Budapest: KMI Rota Press, 89–94

Phillips, P 1989 'Flint procurement in prehistoric quarry ditches', *in* Brooks, I and Phillips, P (eds) *Breaking the Stony Silence: Papers from the Sheffield Lithics Conference 1988* (Brit Archaeol Rep, British Series **213**). Oxford: Brit Archaeol Rep, 33–52

Phillips, P, Field, F N, and Taylor, G V 1990 'Bronze age cemeteries and flint industries from Salmonby'. *Lincolnshire Hist Archaeol,* **25**, 5–11

Piggott, S 1954 *Neolithic Cultures of the British Isles.* Cambridge: Cambridge University Press

Piggott, S 1983 'Archaeological Retrospect 5'. *Antiquity* **57**, 28–36

Pitt Rivers, A H L F 1884 'Address of Major-General Pitt-Rivers to the Antiquarian Section at the annual meeting of the Institute, held at Lewes'. *Archaeol J* **41**, 58–78

Pitts, M 1996 'The stone axe in Britain'. *Proc Prehist Soc* **62**, 311–72

Plowright, C B 1891 'Neolithic man in west Norfolk'. *Trans Norfolk Norwich Natur Soc* **5** (1889–94), 250–64

Posnansky, M, 1963. 'The Lower and Middle Palaeolithic industries of the East Midlands'. *Proc Prehist Soc* **29**, 357–94

Powell, J A 1920 'Implements from Beer Head, Devon'. *Proc Prehist Soc East Anglia* **3**, 208–9

Pull, J H 1932 *The Flint Miners of Blackpatch.* London: Williams and Norgate

Pull, J H 1933a 'Some discoveries at Findon: no 2, the fire mound.' *Sussex County Mag,* **7** (8: August), 506–8

Pull, J H 1933b 'Some discoveries at Findon: no. 6, the flint mines'. *Sussex County Mag* **7** (12: December), 810–14

Pull, J H 1935 'The stone age villages of Downland: no 1, the discovery of Neolithic settlements in West Sussex'. *Sussex County Mag* **9** (7: July), 437–9

Pull, J H 1953 'Further discoveries at Church Hill, Findon'. *Sussex County Mag* **27** (1: January), 15–21

Pull, J H and Sainsbury, C E 1928 'The round barrows of Blackpatch: articles 1–8'. *Worthing Herald/Herald Magazine,* April 21, April 28, May 5, May 12, May 26, June 9, June 16, June 23, July 14 1928

Pull, J H and Sainsbury, C E 1929 'The flint miners of Blackpatch: article no 5, the dwellings and hut sites'. *Worthing Herald/Herald Magazine,* June 1, 1929

Pye, E M 1968. 'The flint mines at Blackpatch, Church Hill and Cissbury, Sussex. A report on the late J H Pull's excavations 1922–1955'. Unpublished MA dissertation, University of Edinburgh

Ratcliffe-Densham, H B A and Ratcliffe-Densham, M M 1953 'A Celtic farm on Blackpatch'. *Sussex Archaeol Collect* **91**, 69–83.

Richards, J 1990 *The Stonehenge Environs Project* (English Heritage Archaeol Rep **16**). London: Historic Buildings and Monuments Commission for England

Ride, D J 1998 'Excavation of a linear earthwork and flint mines at Martin's Clump, Over Wallop, Hampshire, 1984'. *Proc Hampshire Fld Club Archaeol Soc* **53**, 1–23

Ride, D J, and James, D J 1989 'An account of the prehistoric flint mine at Martin's Clump, Over Wallop, Hampshire. 1954–5'. *Proc Hampshire Fld Club Archaeol Soc* **45**, 213–15

Roberts, M B, Stringer, C B, and Parfitt, S A 1994 'A hominid tibia from Middle Pleistocene sediments at Boxgrove'. *UK Nature* **369**, 311–13

Rolleston, G 1879 'Notes on skeleton found at Cissbury, April, 1878'. *J Anthropol Inst* **8**, 377–89

Rowe, A W 1903 'The zones of the white chalk of the English coast: III Devon'. *Proc Geol Ass* **18**, 1–52

Russell, M forthcoming *Excavations by J H Pull at the Prehistoric Flint-mining Sites of Blackpatch, Church Hill, Cissbury and Tolmere, Findon, West Sussex, 1922–1955.* Bournemouth University, School of Conservation Sciences, Occasional Papers. Bournemouth: Bournemouth University, School of Conservation Sciences

Salisbury, E F 1961 'Prehistoric flint-mines on Long Down'. *Sussex Archaeol Collect* **99**, 66–73

Saville, A 1995 'Prehistoric exploitation of flint from the Buchan Ridge Gravels, Grampian Region, north-east Scotland'. *Archaeologia Polonia* **33**, 353–68

Sellwood, B W 1984. 'The rock-types represented in the town wall at Silchester'. In Fulford, M *Silchester: Excavations on the Defences 1974–80* (Britannia Monograph Series **5**). London: Society for the Promotion of Roman Studies, 224–30

Shennan, S J, Healy, F and Smith I F 1985 'The excavation of a ring-ditch at Tye Field, Lawford, Essex'. *Archaeol J* **142**, 150–215

Sheppard, T 1920 'The origin of the materials used in the manufacture of prehistoric stone weapons in east Yorkshire'. *Trans East Riding Antiq Soc* **23**, 34–54

Shepherd, W 1972 *Flint: Its Origins, Properties and Uses.* London: Faber and Faber

Sieveking, G de G 1979 'Grime's Graves and prehistoric European flint mining', *in* Crawford, H (ed) *Subterranean Britain: Aspects of Underground Archaeology.* London: Baker 1–43

Sieveking, G de G, Bush, P, Ferguson, J, Craddock, P T, Hughes, M J and Cowell, M R 1972 'Prehistoric flint mines and their identification as sources of raw material'. *Archaeometry* **14**, 151–76

Sieveking, G de G, Longworth, I H, Hughes, M S, Clark, A J and Millett, M 1973 'A new survey of Grime's Graves'. *Proc Prehist Soc* **39**, 182–218

Skertchley, S B J 1879. 'On the manufacture of gunflints, the methods of excavating for flint, the age of palaeolithic man, and the connexion (sic) between Neolithic art and the gunflint trade'. *Memoirs of the Geological Survey of England and Wales.* London: HMSO

Smith, I F 1979 'The chronology of British stone implements', *in* Clough T H McK and Cummins W A (eds) *Stone Axe Studies* (Counc Brit Archaeol Res Rep **23**). London: Counc Brit Archaeol, 13–22

Smith, R A 1912 'On the date of Grime's Graves and Cissbury flint mines'. *Archaeologia* **63**, 109–58

Spurrell, F C J 1880 'Account of Neolithic flint mines at Crayford, Kent'. *Archaeol J* **37**, 332–5

Spurrell, F C J 1881 'Deneholes and artificial caves with vertical entrances'. *Archaeol J* **38**, 391–409

Spurrell, F C J 1883 'On some large collections of shallow pits in Norfolk and elsewhere'. *Archaeol J* **40**, 281–95

Stoertz, C 1997 *Ancient Landscapes of the Yorkshire Wolds: Aerial Photographic Transcription and Analysis.* Swindon: Royal Commission on the Historical Monuments of England

Stone, J F S 1931a 'Easton Down, Winterslow, S Wilts, Flint Mine excavation, 1930'. *Wiltshire Archaeol Mag* **45**, 350–72

Stone, J F S 1931b 'A settlement site of the Beaker period on Easton Down, Winterslow, S Wilts'. *Wiltshire Archaeol Mag* **45**, 366–72

Stone, J F S 1933a 'A Middle Bronze Age urnfield on Easton Down, Winterslow'. *Wiltshire Archaeol Mag* **46**, 218–24

Stone, J F S 1933b 'Excavations at Easton Down, Winterslow 1931–32'. *Wiltshire Archaeol Mag* **46**, 225–42

Stone, J F S 1933c 'A flint mine at Martin's Clump, Over Wallop'. *Proc Hampshire Fld Club Archaeol Soc* **12** (2), 177–80

Stone, J F S 1935 'Excavations at Easton Down, Winterslow 1933–4'. *Wiltshire Archaeol Mag* **47**, 68–80

Stuiver, M, and Reimer, P J 1986 'A computer program for radiocarbon age calculation'. *Radiocarbon* **28**, 1022–30

Sturge, W A 1908 'The polished axe found by Canon Greenwell in a flint pit at Grime's Graves'. *Man* **8**, 166–8

Thomas, J 1993 'Discourse, Totalization and "the Neolithic"'. In Tilley, C (ed) *Interpretative Archaeology.* Oxford: Berg, 357–94

Thomas, K D 1982 'Neolithic enclosures and woodland habitats on the South Downs in Sussex, England', *in* Bell, M and Limbrey, S (eds) *Archaeological Aspects of Woodland Ecology* (Brit Archaeol Rep, International Series **146**). Oxford: Brit Archaeol Rep, 147–70

Thomas, M S 1997. 'A Neolithic axe from Windover Hill'.

Sussex Archaeol Collect, **135**, 300-01

Tilley, C 1994 *A Phenomenology of Landscape.* Oxford: Berg

Tingle, C 1998 *The Prehistory of Beer Head* (Brit Archaeol Rep, British Series **270**). Oxford: Brit Archaeol Rep

Todd, K R U 1949 'A neolithic flint mine at east Horsley'. *Surrey Archaeol Collect* **51**, 142–3 and plate xviii(a)

Turner, Rev E 1850 'On the military earthworks of the South Downs, with a more enlarged account of Cissbury, one of the principal of them'. *Sussex Archaeol Collect* **3**, 173–84

Wade, A G 1922. 'Ancient flint mines at Stoke Down, Sussex'. *Proc Prehist Soc East Anglia* **4**, 82–91

Wainwright, G J and Longworth, I H 1971. *Durrington Walls: Excavations 1966–1968* (Rep Res Comm Soc Antiq London **29**). London: Soc Antiq London

Warren, S H 1919 'A stone axe factory at Graig Lwyd, Penmaenmawr'. *J Roy Anthropol Inst* **49**, 342–65

Welch, M G 1983. *Early Anglo-Saxon Sussex* (Brit Archaeol Rep, British Series **112**). Oxford: Brit Archaeol Rep

White, S 1995 'A most lovable character'. *Sussex Past and Present* **11** (Dec 1995)

Whittle, A 1995 'Gifts from the earth: symbolic dimensions of the use and production of Neolithic flint and stone axes'. *Archaeologia Polona* **33**, 247–60

Whittle, A 1996 *Europe in the Neolithic: The Creation of New Worlds.* Cambridge: Cambridge University Press

Willett, E H 1875 'On flint workings at Cissbury, Sussex'. *Archaeologia* **65**, 337–48

Williams, J H 1971 'Roman building materials in south-east England'. *Britannia* **2**, 166–95

Wood, E S 1952 'Neolithic Sites in West Surrey'. *Surrey Archaeol Collect* **52**, 11–28 and plates i-iv

Woods, G M 1925 'A surface site in south east Devon'. *Proc Prehist Soc East Anglia* **5**, 83–5

Woods, G M 1929 'A Stone Age site in south east Devon'. *Proc Devon Archaeol Exploration Soc* **1**, 10–14

Woodward, A B, and Woodward, P J 1996 'The topography of some barrow cemeteries in Bronze Age Wessex'. *Proc Prehist Soc* **62**, 275–92

Woolworth, A R 1983 'The Red Pipestone Quarry of Minnesota'. *The Minnesota Archaeologist* **42** (1 and 2)

Wright, T 1885 *The Celt, the Roman and the Saxon: a History of the Early Inhabitants of Britain .....* London: Trübner and Co

Young, R 1984 'Potential sources of flint and chert in the north-east of England'. *Lithics* **5**, 3–9

Index